GUIDELINES FOR CHRISTIAN
THEOLOGY IN AFRICA

GUIDELINES
FOR CHRISTIAN THEOLOGY
IN AFRICA

Osadolor Imasogie

AFRICA CHRISTIAN PRESS

Published by the
  Africa Christian Press
  PO Box 30
  Achimota, Ghana, West Africa

First Edition

ISBN 0-9964-87-512-6

Phototypeset in England by
Nuprint Services Ltd, Harpenden, Herts.

CONTENTS

FOREWORD

Writing about the contextualization of Christian theology is now in vogue among Western Christians working in cross-cultural contexts and increasingly among non-Western church leaders. It's about time. For though the theologians have always done their work in response to at least certain of the questions raised by the world around them, we are just now becoming conscious of this fact. "All theologies are contextually conditioned," says Robert McAfee Brown, and "there is nothing wrong with theology being contextually conditioned."[1]

The contextualization of Christianity is nothing more than the process of interpreting Christian truth in terms of and applying it to the real life issues arising from the sociocultural context within which the interpreters live.[2] It involves taking seriously both every day human life and God's desire to be involved in it. God's involvement in the life of the Hebrews throughout the Old Testament demonstrates his commitment to contextualization. So does Jesus' involvement with the people of his day and his willingness to deal with their concerns and questions. Paul and the other New Testament authors, likewise, contextualized God's messages for the people to whom they wrote.

The fact that the authors of Scripture are contextualizing for different audiences explains the surface level differences between the messages of, say, James and Paul or Paul and Jesus or the Old Testament and the New Testament. At a deeper level these messages are a part of the same overall Message. But the application of that Message to the felt needs of different people in different contexts often makes it look different, especially at first glance.

But there is within Scripture the problem of the Judaizers. These Hebrew Christians had come rightly to understand the Gospel as applying to their cultural context. But they then went on to assume that the Gospel also endorsed their culture, That is, they believed that since God was willing to enter their way of life he was, therefore, endorsing that way as the only valid cultural expression. These Judaizers concluded that since God required circumcision and other Hebrew religious ritual as the appropriate response of Hebrew people to himself, he would naturally expect Gentiles who responded to the Christian message to learn and practice these customs too. They absolutized their Jewish ways of thinking and behaving as God's prescribed ways. They, therefore, imposed these ways on their Gentile converts whenever they had the power to do so. Paul's stance was, however, against the Judaizers' approach and in favour of contextualization (see Acts 15:1–34; 1 Corinthians 9:19–22).

The history of Christianity since New Testament times has, however, seen a constant tendency to revert to the Judaizers' approach on the part of the splitting group that the "orthodox" system is not meeting the heresy trials of the early centuries A.D. or the Reformation or the Wesleyan split from Anglicanism or any of the subsequent splits within Western Christianity or the contemporary missionary movement, the pattern is the same: the group in power gets to define orthodoxy and to impose it on less powerful groups unless and until the latter develop enough strength to separate from the dominating group. When such splits take place, then there is usually some valid contention on the part of the splitting group that the "orthodox" system is not meeting the needs of the constituency that they represent. They seek, therefore, to contextualize Christianity for that group.

It is characteristic of groups in power –whether the power is political or theological and whether the group in power is well or poorly motivated – not to notice the injustice they are perpetrating. Generations of highly motivated, sincere, well-meaning missionaries, for example, have seldom seen themselves as oppressors. Indeed, they have often seen themselves as giving "their" people "God's very best" – meaning, of course, what they the missionaries considered to be the best from their point of view. Given the cultural differences between missionaries and the Africans, Asians, Latin Americans, etc. among whom they worked, then, what was given frequently "scratched the receivers where they didn't itch." Even the best of Western theological thinking has been found by non-Westerners to be answering questions that they are simply not asking, while completely ignoring questions about which they are desperately concerned.

Increasingly, however, both perceptive missionaries and the church leaders of non-Western lands are asking questions such as, "If Christianity is universally valid, does it not have answers to the questions non-Westerners are asking?" "Cannot the Bible be properly interpreted outside of the academic ghettos of Europe and America?" And the experiments being conducted in many parts of the world are pointing ever more positively to the appropriateness of developing genuinely Christian theologizing within non-Western cultural contexts.

This brief book by Dr. Imasogie is a worthy contribution to the growing literature on this subject by Africans themselves. It is a call for relevant Christian theologizing from an African base. This call is built upon a critique of what I term a "Judaizers'" approach to theologizing — that is, the imposition on Africans of theology that has been "made in Euromerica" by those in power on the assumption that that theology is absolute. Far from being absolute, Dr. Imasogie contends that even Western theology is the result of contextualization — but to a Western world view.

The author, therefore, draws a series of contrasts between Western and African world view assumptions. Though the biblical basis for theological reflection is to be the same for the proponents of each world view, the output may be quite different (at least at certain points) due to the sometimes wide divergence between the basic assumptions in terms of which that reflection is done.

In his final chapter, then, Dr. Imasogie provides us with a series of guidelines for a new approach to theologizing from an African world view base. Among these are a call for what I would call a "theology of power" based on a new awareness of the place of the Holy Spirit and the "sacramental nature of the universe." Such foci would fill at the intellectual level a number of the blanks in Western theologies. At the practice level, then, such an approach paves the way for "power encounters"[3] where the forces of evil are actually confronted and tested by the power of God (as in the days of Moses and Elijah) in physical healing and other concrete demonstrations of God's power. Such practical applications have been missing from most Western theologizing for a long time, though they are prominent in the Bible.

From a book like this Africans can receive encouragement and guidance in their quest for Christian theological self-hood. There is much here to be pondered, probed, experimented with and expanded upon by committed Africans. We in the West, then, can learn much about where concerned Africans are itching and how at least one of them goes about dealing with such itches. It is clear that we are blocked at points by our Western world view(s) from really feeling some of the kinds of things that Dr. Imasogie speaks of, based as they are on a radically different approach to reality. Nevertheless, the venture into theological waters by Africans needs the sympathetic understanding and support of as many of us as possible. And we stand to gain new insights both into the Bible and into ourselves. All of us from the West who have opened ourselves up to experiencing Africa have come away the richer for it.

This is not the last word on the subject but it is a very helpful one. I am happy to play a small part in bringing it to public attention.

Charles H. Kraft
Pasadena, California

PREFACE

The urge to write this book was generated several years ago. The need to do so became clear as I, like other parish pastors, grappled with the fears and reactions of African Christians in times of existential crisis. We observed that the usual resort of the average African Christian in crisis situations is a reversion to traditional African religious practices. I dismissed the urge to write at the time, however, partly because I did not feel competent to embark on such a project and partly because I was not sure if the observed reaction was universal in Africa or simply a local phenomenon.

Now, however, after several years as a teacher of ministerial students, my doubts concerning the pervasiveness of the reaction among Christians have disappeared. Through my interactions with professional colleagues who attend the annual conferences of the West African Association of Theological Institutions (WAATI) and the questions raised by my students I have become convinced that my parish experience has unearthed a major and widespread problem.

The universality of the problem among African Christians, as established from these contacts, led me to the suspicion that there might be some defects in the apologetic approach taught by the Christian missionaries as well as in the broader formulation of Christian theology. It is against this background that I decided to spend my Sabbatical leave (1977–78) in studying theological methodology at the Divinity School of Vanderbilt University in Nashville, Tennessee, U.S.A.

I chose this area of study with the hope that an exposure to the presuppositions underlying the various theological methodologies would lead me to discover better guidelines for relevant Christian theologizing in Africa. I was fortunate to have Professor Edward Farley as my Faculty Advisor during that year. Professor Farley is a professor of theology. Through his able guidance my suspicion was confirmed that both theological perception and formulation are significantly culturally conditioned. It became clear that failure to come to grips with this reality has tended to make orthodox Christian theological formulations irrelevant to the needs of contemporary Christians in many cultures. New theologies have thus emerged in protest against the inability of traditional Western Christian theologians to re-examine their presuppositions in the light of new situations. Without such re-examination such theologians have become insensitive to divine activity on the modern historical scene.

The observed lack of total commitment of the average African Christian to Christ is due to the lack of "fit" between Christian theology and African life. This lack of fit is, in turn, due to this same failure of Western orthodox theologians to take African world views into consideration in their theological formulations. In the absence of such an existential fit between theology and life, the African reverts to his traditional practices in times of serious problems. The thrust of the arguments in this book is to make a case that if Christian theology is to be relevant for the African his world view and self-understanding must be taken into account. This effort will necessitate the evolving of new guidelines for Christian theologizing in Africa.

In writing this book, I am indebted to the intellectual brilliance and warm human relations of Professor Farley. Professor Farley's interest did not stop with the end of my sabbatical leave. He took time to read and make incisive comments, suggestions on and criticism of the first draft which I mailed to him for that purpose. He did not agree with some of my views, but as much as possible his suggestions, comments and criticism have been taken into account in the final product. Needless to say, I alone take full responsibility for any deficiencies.

My desire to write the book would, perhaps, not have come to fruition if the Nigerian Baptist Theological Seminary had not granted me a sabbatical leave. For that act of kindness, I am grateful to the Board of Governors, the former Principal, Dr. C. F. Whirley, and the Faculty of the Institution for making it possible for me to be on leave for one academic year. My special thanks go to my wife who shouldered the family responsibilities during my absence. My thanks also go to my colleague, Miss Mary Jane Whorton, who proof-read the manuscripts and to Mrs Felicia O. Omoni who transcribed my hardly legible handwriting into typewritten form. I am, finally, grateful to Professor Kraft for editing the manuscript and for his kind Foreword.

It only remains for me to say that the effort made here is only a modest attempt to peep into a deep and complex problem which defies simple solution. It is hoped that the questions raised will engender fresh interest in the study of theological methodology. It is my conviction that only such a course of study will enable us to unearth the presuppositions underlying various theological schools of thought and the contextual factors that shape these presuppositions and the resultant perception and theological formulation of religious experience.

Osadolor Imasogie
Nigeria

1

AN INCARNATIONAL RELIGION

Fundamental to the thesis of this book is the assumption that Christianity is an incarnational religion. Christian theology must, therefore, be informed by the contextual milieu of its target audience in such a way that the Word will become flesh among the people. It is our view that the average African Christian's commitment to Christ is superficial because the current formulation of Christian theology fails to take cognizance of this fundamental fact. The superficiality of the African Christian's commitment is evidenced by the fact that when he is faced with problems and uncertainties he often reverts to traditional religious practices. This will be elaborated upon later.

This first chapter will attempt to substantiate the assumption that Christianity is an incarnational religion. On the basis of this discussion we will argue that the superficiality of the average African's commitment to Christ is the result of the failure of Christian theologians to take the African context seriously. In chapter two it will be shown that theology is contextually influenced. Chapter three argues that since theological perception is contextually conditioned, the difference between Western world views and those typical of much of Africa renders the othodox (i.e. Western) formulations of Christian theology less relevant for the African. This is because his world view and consequent self-understanding have not received serious consideration by orthodox theologians. On the basis of the foregoing chapters, the last chapter presents guidelines for developing Christian theology in Africa. This is the background against which the present chapter, which treats Christianity as an incarnational religion, must be read.

Christianity is the outcome of the existential response of faith of the early believers to the saving Presence of God in the God-man, Jesus Christ. That saving Presence was radiated through life, ministry, death, the resurrection and ascension of the historical Jesus of Nazareth, the Incarnate Word of God.

By the end of the first century, that initial response of faith had come to be summarized in different forms, the most typical of which is recorded in the opening of John's gospel:

> Before the world was created, the Word already existed; he was with God, and he was the same as God. From the very beginning the Word was with God. Through him God made all things; not one thing in all creation was made without him. The Word had life in himself, and this life brought light to men. The light shines in the darkness, and the darkness has never put it out.
>
> God sent his messenger, a man named John, who came to tell people about the light. He came to tell them, so that all should hear the message and believe....
>
> The Word, then, was in the world. God made the world through him, yet the world did not know him. He came to his own country, but his own people did not receive him. Some, however, did receive him and believed in him; so he gave them the right to become God's children. They did not become God's children by natural means, by being born as the children of a human father; God himself was their Father.
>
> The Word became a human being and lived among us. We saw his glory, full of grace and truth. This was the glory which he received as the Father's only Son (John 1:1–14, TEV).

Two important facts must be noted in this classic expression of the human apprehension of the Saving Presence of God in the Christ-event. First, in the human Jesus of Nazareth, the Eternal God or Christ was incarnated in order that he might be apprehended by the creatures whom he created. Second, in spite of the many years during which God chose and prepared the Jews for this very historical self-disclosure, the bulk of the people did not recognize the divine Presence when it became incarnate in their midst in the person of Jesus of Nazareth. However, a few of the Jews, looking at the man, Jesus, saw beyond his human flesh and blood. These few men were able, under the influence of God's power, to testify that behind the facade of this humanness was God himself. If I may repeat part of what has been stated:

> The Word became a human being and lived among us. We saw his glory, full of grace and truth. This was the glory which he received as the Father's only Son (John 1:14, TEV).

As John wrote many years later:

> We write to you about the Word of life, which has existed from the very beginning: we have heard it, and we have seen it with our eyes; yes, we have seen it, and our hands have touched it. When this life became visible, we saw it; so we speak of it and tell you about the eternal life which was with the Father and was made known to us (I John 1:1–2, TEV).

One may ask: Why was it that God decided to become incarnate in Jesus of Nazareth to be initially apprehended by a particular people at a particular time in history? Why did he decide that, through this people, his self-disclosure would be made known to the rest of the world? That being so, why was it that the bulk of these chosen people, despite many years of preparation, did not recognize his saving Presence when he did manifest it in a concrete human medium? No one can answer these questions with any air of finality. But whatever form the answers may take, they must revolve around the hiddenness of God and the mystery of his Being. The answers may also take into account man's inability to think in the abstract which necessitates the need for a concrete medium of revelation.

Role of culture
In addition to the points listed above, any attempt to answer the questions raised must take note of the role of culture in human perception. No human perception is pure; every perception is tainted by the distorting effect of one's culture. Added to this is the bane of

human inclination to equate the symbols of divine meditation with the divine reality itself. God is the Eternal Presence to be recognized only as He makes himself known through human beings, situations and material symbols. The structure of the human mind being what it is, man under subtle cultural influences invariably tends to equate the medium of revelation with divine Reality. The end result is that the divine Presence is distorted and misplaced beneath the cultural overlay which is the culminative reality of the historical experience and aspirations of the people involved.

This was the process that created problems for the Jews as a people in their encounter with God incarnate in the historical Jesus of Nazareth. Those among them who discerned the Presence of God in Jesus were those who were able to transcend these subtle influences. This is the point of Matthew 16:16–18 where, following Peter's declaration of his recognition of the saving Presence of God in Jesus, Jesus is quoted as saying:

> Simon son of Jonah, you are favoured indeed! You did not learn that from mortal man; it was revealed to you by my heavenly Father (NEB).

The Gospel record of Jesus' obvious hesitation to accept the title of Messiah unless it was qualified can only be understood against the background of the cultural distortion of perception which has been described above. At the time of Jesus' ministry in the flesh, many years of political oppression had caused the Jews to lose sight of the spiritual nature of the promised Messiah and of their own divine mission as heralds of God's saving Presence. Instead they were looking for a political Messiah who would free them politically and economically from their oppressors. Consequently, given such preoccupation with political freedom, they could only understand their religion in terms of the nation. The result was that the term Messiah, which was a symbol of the availability of God's saving Presence in their midst, came to be identified with a national military hero. By the same process, the temple, the law and the rituals came to be regarded as the embodiments of God in their midst. In consequence, they failed to recognize the Messiah who did not fit into their national aspirations and who did not accept the accidentals of their religion which they had come to absolutize.

Thus the early Jewish Christians were those who were enabled, because of their openness to God, to transcend their cultural barriers to spiritual apprehension and their ancestral interpretations of their religious symbols. As a result of such transcendence they were able to discern, in Jesus, that saving divine Presence. The reality of this discernment is capsuled in the confession already quoted.

In other words, they saw in Jesus of Nazareth God's solution to the deeper problems of oppression, human sin, anxiety and death. Put in another way, the initial Jewish Christians found in Jesus *salvation* understood in terms of *wholeness*. Peter expressed this succinctly, when, in answer to Jesus' question at a most critical point in his ministry, he declared: "Lord, to whom would we go? You have the words that give eternal life. And now we believe and know that you are the Holy One from God" (John 6:68–69, TEV).

The same saving Presence of God in Christ is forever available to people of all generations and cultures as they respond in faith to the Risen Lord who is no longer limited by space and time. This eternal availability of God's saving Presence in Christ is still rooted in the historical incarnation, for it was there that God concretized his salvation in historical terms. However, the very fact of historical incarnation suggests that this Presence is not always *effectively* mediated through the medium of theology formulated in one culture, nor through the religious symbols devised in one culture and generation. Symbols lose their potency and the theological formulations become atrophied when the symbols around which they are built have become irrelevant or foreign to a people of another culture. There is always a search for living and relevant symbols that mediate the saving Presence of God in Jesus Christ. This is what the theologians mean by the concept of the contemporaneity of the eternal Christ who comes in every age and culture to every generation waiting to be apprehended in the cultural and historical life situation of a particular people. He does not become real to the people merely on the basis of what an earlier generation and culture has said, as important and valid as this is. He becomes real only on the basis of the authentic discernment by every generation. When this discernment occurs the new generation discovers, to its joy, that the Christ thus disclosed is the same eternal Christ known by the earlier generation and culture in their own situation.

The early church Fathers, in their numerous church councils set up to formulate their understanding of Christ in the language and culture of the non-Christian world, demonstrated their acceptance of this principle. One would have thought that Christian theologians in Africa would borrow a leaf from their forebears in this regard. This was, unfortunately, not to be for many years. To the best of my knowledge, the need to take the cultural milieu into account in the formulation of Christian theology in foreign fields was not officially recognized until 1952. In that year the International Missionary Council meeting in Willengen signified its awareness of this necessity in the following declaration:

> While the church of Christ in any place and at any time must exhibit the marks without which it will not be a Church, it has the responsibility to exhibit them in a distinct way, incorporating into the service of Christ whatever heritage of cultural values it may have been given by God's grace. This is not being rooted in the soil but related to the soil. The Church can only be rooted in Christ. But the Gospel must be so presented to the men and women that its contemporary and compelling relevance is recognized. It cannot be recognized as long as it disappears in a foreign guise, imitating and producing the characteristics of a church in some remote and alien land. Foreign, in one sense, the church must always be; its citizenship is in heaven and it is an agent of transformation. [1]

Contrary to expectations, no serious effort has been made to implement the implications of that declaration in Africa. It was only twenty-one years later at a consultation on The Inner Dialogue with Primal World-views[2] held in Ibadan, Nigeria, in 1973, that Christian theologians in Africa re-examined the problem. This was followed by a book entitled *African Christian Theology – Adaptation or Incarnation?*[3] One wonders what has been the cause of hesitancy to carry on Christian theologizing within the framework of African world views, a procedure which was accepted as normal by early Christians! Perhaps the traditional Christian's negative attitude to other religions and world views has been responsible for the lack of enthusiasm in this regard.

To avoid any misunderstanding it must be made clear from the outset that there is no intention here to argue in a parochial way for a particular Christian theology for Africa. Theology, if it is authentic, must participate in universality. However, the aim is to stress that no theology is authentic and universal if it does not meet the integrated needs of a particular people in a particular historical context. For the

Word must become flesh in a given culture and context in order to be genuinely and meaningfully apprehended wholeheartedly. It is only as theology responds to the existential needs of a people within the specific cultural and historical milieu of their self-understanding that the universal of it can be enhanced and enriched. After all, what is universality if it does not mean relevance for people concerned? Relevance has meaning only in terms of meeting the vital needs of a people. This cannot happen in a contextual vacuum. This concept of universality is a far cry from the often lopsided theology that masquerades as universal. This is so because most theologians are not even aware of the underlying forces that shape the theological formulations that they wrongly assume to have universal application. The significance of this observation will emerge in due course.

Meaning of theology

This leads us then to questions such as the meaning of the term theology, its task, sources and norm. Of one piece with these questions is the problem of hermeneutic principles in theologizing. These are points that must be clearly delineated in the course of this work. But in the meantime we will address ourselves to the meaning of the word theology. Theology has been defined in different ways by different writers – each one stressing the aspect that fits his scheme. For our purpose here we will follow Paul Tillich's definition. For him, "theology is the statement of the truth of the Christian message and interpretation of this truth for every generation."[4] Tillich goes on to add that "theology moves back and forth between two poles, the eternal truth of its foundation and the temporal situation in which the eternal truth must be received."[5] Note that this definition takes a serious view of the divine and human – the eternal and temporal – elements in theologizing. Theology is an explication of the eternal truth – the Christian message – namely, that God was in Christ reconciling the world to himself. This, as we have already indicated, is the testimony of the first witnesses to the historical self-disclosure of God in Jesus, the Christ.

The above definition of theology not only emphasizes the divine source of theology, it also underscores the temporal situation in which the eternal Presence must be discerned, appropriated by and interpreted for each generation. In other words, the eternal reality must become flesh, as it were, in every situation and in each generation. Without this no generation in its peculiar human experience can come into existential grips with the reality and meaning of Christ in its temporal *here* and *now*. This is in line with the history of Christian thought, but we so often forget. Theology is never to be done in a cultural vacuum. Much of the history of Christian doctrine is a commentary on the struggle between Jewish thought patterns and the Greek world view vis-a-vis the existential apprehension of the Christ within these thought-patterns. It is noteworthy to know that as Cobb expresses it, "In the long run, it was Greek and not Jewish Christianity that triumphed; hence it was the problems of relating Greek thought to Christian faith that determined much of the intellectual history of Christendom."[6] Of course, Cobb here refers to the basic strands in Christian doctrine which have been interpreted and reinterpreted in every generation with varying emphases and colourings as determined by historical realities in the light of divine Presence.

It is clear from what has been said that no theologian begins his theologizing without certain presuppositions concerning such things as the source and norms for theology and the concrete human experience to which he seeks to relate the meaning of Christ. The tragedy, as already explained, is that in most cases the theologian is not consciously aware of these presuppositions, especially when he leaves one cultural environment for another. The fact remains that whether he is aware or not his methodology is shaped by his cultural upbringing, his traditional convictions and his intuitive insights. All these subtly condition his choice of norm and hermeneutical principles in his theologizing.

Theological methodology

In view of the foregoing, it is imperative for every theologian to enunciate clearly his theological methodology and the presuppositions that lead him to that choice. As Farley points out, theological methodology as suggested above did not feature prominently in the theologies of the early Christian theologians.[7] It was not that they were absent, but they were not explicitly stated because the need was not felt. For one thing, they were writing, for the most part, within a homogeneous group under the assumption that they believed basically the same thing. The audience was presumed to be religious and actively conscious of divine reality and to have accepted the Scriptures without any serious questions about the orthodox interpretation. This apparent state of innocence was soon to be shaken by the Reformation which, among other things, pointed to the need to specify clearly the criteria for theology. Thus, for the first time after the initial crystallization of Christian doctrine as a result of its encounter with Greek thought patterns, the Reformation raised questions about the nature of Christianity in its doctrinal expression. By implication questions were raised about the place of the Scriptures over against the traditional interpretations handed down by the Church Fathers. Where does the ultimate authority reside in the theological formulation of Faith? Does it reside in the Scriptures or in tradition as interpreted by the Church Fathers? These were the crucial questions for the Reformers. The answers to these questions determined, for the Reformers, the major difference between Protestantism and Roman Catholicism.

This need for a concise statement on theological methodology has been further heightened by the more recent impact of the successive waves of the historical-critical method in biblical studies, the post-historical method, the rise of secularism and the recent awareness of the need to secure political and economic emancipation for the oppressed. The need for political emancipation of the Blacks in the United States of America and South Africa and the economic emancipation of the oppressed in Latin America have forced theologians to re-examine their presuppositions. This becomes necessary because in the face of the mounting revolutionary movements, the orthodox theological formulations become embarrassingly impotent and irrelevant. The new self-understanding of the oppressed calls for a new way of viewing theological relevance in their struggle for humanization in the context of the Christian message of love and brotherhood of man irrespective of colour and social status. The upshot of these undercurrents has been the multiplicity of brands of theology which have mushroomed in our time. A summary of some of these theologies and the presuppositions that brought them into being will be presented in the next chapter.

It must be emphatically stated that the purpose of this work is not to get on the bandwagon of new theologies. The reference to the new theologies and the subsequent explication of a selected number of them is to show that there comes a time when traditional approaches to theologizing, and to anything for that matter, no longer meet human needs. At such a time it is wise to re-examine the situation in order to identify the problems and, on the basis of the findings, to grapple with the new directions indicated. As already pointed out, the need to do theology that takes the African context into account is long overdue.

Historically, Christianity was brought to Sub-Saharan Africa after it had taken definite form in the West. As we have implied in our earlier reference to the history of Christian thought, when Christianity was being planted in the West via Asia Minor the faith was still in a fluid state. The framework of the theology brought from the West to Africa, however, was set, forged in the interaction between the original Jewish world view and that of the Greeks and later Europeans. After over a thousand years of its existence in the West and with all the cultural baggage that had accrued during that time, Christianity was introduced to Sub-Saharan Africa. Since the set formulations of Western Christianity were by then taken for granted without conscious awareness of the historical development of its doctrinal formulations and the cultural influences that had shaped them, the Western heralds felt no need to take the African context into consideration in their presentations.

In addition, there was, probably, the unfortunate belief that theology was closed instead of being open-ended. The church dogmatic tradition formulation came to be regarded as if it were a fossilized distillation of the deposit of divine revelation. Such a concept of theological formulation beclouds the dynamic nature of Christ who promises to continue to reveal God to us in every human situation through the continuing activity of the Holy Spirit. Lack of sensitivity to the dynamic nature of the theological enterprise made most missionaries unresponsive to the world view and self-understanding of the Africans they encountered, as well as the role of culture in perception that results from that world view. The result of this failure is that, underneath the appearance of acceptance and understanding, Christianity, for many Africans, remains a foreign religion. The sad implication is that many Africans have not accepted Christianity completely as the all-sufficient religion that meets *all* human needs. The truth of this assertion is borne out by the fact that in times of existential crisis many respectable African Christians revert to traditional religious practices as the means for meeting their spiritual needs. This point will be discussed in detail in the final chapter of this book.

It does not require much argument to establish the fact that for religion to be valid it must pervade the whole of human existence if it is to meet man's needs as he understands them. Since a person's self-understanding is tied up with his world view, it is crucial that a Christian evangelist know that world view if there is to be any assurance of success in communicating the Christian message. Without this understanding, a way may not be opened for the Eternal Word to take form and dwell among a people so that they may see his glory as "the glory of the only Son of God" who "existed before all things, and in union with [whom] all things have their proper place" (Colossians 1:17, TEV). It is only when this incarnation takes place that Christianity ceases to be seen as a foreign religion. Christ is then not regarded as a 'stranger-god' who does not know how to handle those crises with which the white man is not familiar. Instead, he is accepted as the one who "is supreme over every spiritual ruler and authority" (Colossians 2:10, TEV), and hence able to save to the uttermost those who are incorporated into him.

The African may not come to this understanding of Christ unless Christ is presented to him from the perspective of his world view. This is what we mean by insisting that Christ, the Eternal Word, must once again, as it were, become incarnate in the culture and thought patterns of the people if he is not to be seen as a foreign god who is unacquainted with the local metaphysical problems of the African.

Our contention throughout this book is that Christianity is the universal religion which only becomes an authentic religion for a particular people when their world view and self-understanding within that world view are taken seriously as they are confronted with the claims of Christ. Failure to do this, invariably, leads to ambivalence in their Christian commitments, especially in times of crisis. The need to prevent such an ambivalence is the reason for this book. In order to further heighten the need to take certain presuppositions in the African context into account in Christian theologizing we shall examine some basic presuppositions of traditional Western Christian theology. This will enable us both to see the inadequacies of those presuppositions and to appreciate the position taken here in suggesting new guidelines for Christian theology in Africa.

2

TRADITIONAL WESTERN CHRISTIAN THEOLOGY AND THE NEW THEOLOGIES

It has already been stated that the purpose of this book is to make a case for a relevant Christian theology in Africa. Such a theology, it has been suggested, must take the African context and world view seriously if the Word is to take flesh in the life and language of the African. In order to lay a solid foundation for this task we need to clear away the traditional Western theological perceptual obstacles that becloud any attempt at a fresh and dynamic perception of the Christ in a new age and circumstance.

The most fruitful way to achieve this purpose, it appears to this writer, is to present some contemporary incisive criticisms of traditional Western Christian theology. The contemporary critics whose views are to be presented here are motivated by the same desire to liberate that theology from its presuppositions that have made it unresponsive to the needs of the new age. Their criticisms will heighten the contention that theology is contextually conditioned and that until this fact is realized, the need for a new approach to Christian theological formulation in Africa and elsewhere may not become possible. Criticism of traditional or orthodox Christian theology is not new. It has often been attacked from various quarters both within and outside of the Church. In response to such attacks theological formulations have been revised from generation to generation. Our primary concern here, however, is with those criticisms made by theologians who are eager to see that the Church, as the agent of Christ, remains radically open to God, on the one hand, and sensitive and responsive to the existential needs of the whole man on the other hand. Unfortunately, the theologians of the

Church, have not always shown such sensitivity. This is not necessarily because they do not desire to do so but because of their unawareness of the presuppositions that often befog their perception of human needs and the discernment of divine solutions to those needs.

In recent years different theologians have sought to pinpoint those cultural and ideological presuppositions that have made it impossible for orthodox theologians to produce relevant theology for contemporary man in his life situation. The attempt to unravel these hidden presuppositions has resulted in the emergence of new theologies, some of which can be rightly called theologies of the left. Some of them, like the radical theology of the early sixties, have no advantage over the orthodox theologies they were intended to correct or replace. These are not worthy of our consideration here. There are, however, several of these new theologians who do succeed in calling attention to some valid flaws in the presuppositions of orthodox theology that demand action. Our initial purpose here is to examine two groups of authentic critics, each operating from a different context with different presuppositions. Their respective criticisms as well as their proposals for new methodologies that are responsive to the life situations of modern man, as seen against the backdrop of divine self-disclosure, will be presented. Our purpose, to repeat, is to provide an introduction to the next chapters of this book. In those chapters, the writer intends to show that if the existential needs of Africans are to be adequately met by the Living Christ there must be new theological guidelines that will take their world views seriously in mediating the claims of Christ.

Our treatment will generate three criticisms – one each from the two groups of theologians to be discussed in this chapter and a third stemming from the Western world view. Each of the two groups of theologians starts with the basic presupposition that all theologies are contextually conditioned. In view of this, one of the groups contends that the failure of traditional theology lies in its inability to reconcile the basic Christian message with the contemporary self-understanding of human existence. This inability is the result of presuppositions that leave no room for the possibility of a new mode of human self-understanding. The other group attributes the irrelevance of traditional theology in meeting the needs of the oppressed to its *de facto* identification of Christianity with the *status quo*. The third issue raising the need for new theological guidelines in the African context is the quasi-scientific world view underlying the traditional Western theological approach. This issue will be taken up in the next chapter.

In the meantime, what has just been said raises some crucial questions concerning the nature of theological presuppositions. These need further elucidation before we embark on the task of validating each of the bases of criticism of the orthodox theology. In the first place, what has been said points up the fact (which is not always consciously acknowledged) that subconscious presuppositions are integral parts of theologizing. Failure to recognize this invariably leads to a grossly distorted perception of divine revelation. Secondly, it calls attention to the subtle manner in which the church dogmatic mentality dominates theologizing rather than an open-ended approach that allows sensitivity to the possibility of divine self-disclosure in a concrete situation. By church dogmatic mentality here is meant the often unconscious acceptance that the divine self-disclosure in the past, present and for all times in all human situations has been exhaustively grasped and embodied in certain confessional dogmatic formulations. All that now remains for the theologian to do in any situation is to bring out the fossilized revelation, as it were, and to use it as a theological sensor to measure the theological meaning of the new experience. The measuring is invariably done in the light of the predetermined perception of the theologian's specific tradition!

This is a static concept of revelation which has no room for the ever fresh dynamism of the living Christ who promised to lead us into all truth in the person of the Holy Spirit. This calls for a renewed emphasis on the need for openness to the leadership of God in any new situation and to be consciously tuned to the possibility of new spiritual insights which God may have in store for those who are tuned to him.

It may be necessary to add that nothing said above should be construed to mean that the basic Christian doctrines as now formulated are invalid *per se*. Nothing could be further from the truth. But it does mean to stress that we do not have the last word yet. The nature of divine revelation is such that further spiritual insights may lead to a deeper and richer understanding of the reality which we now see dimly as through a befogged mirror. The fog which now beclouds our vision may be due to cultural accretions or any other source of influence which needs to be evaporated by the new spiritual insight before we can move closer to the truth. At best our theological formulations are models; not picture models that present realities as they are factually, but disclosure models which are perspectives by means of which we discern and appropriate divine self-disclosure. As perspectives, they are not permanent; they are capable of yielding to better perspectives for understanding revelation. To demonstrate this, a theologian only has to look back into the history of the development of his confessional tradition to see the changes that have taken place in theological understanding. These observable changes attest to the truth of the point we are making here. A most recent example is the Vatican II and its implications for Roman Catholic theology today.

This has been the role of the prophet in the Judeo-Christian religion. His role has been to cause dissatisfaction with the *status quo* in order to arouse the Church from complacency and prepare her for the new things which God is bringing to pass. This is the rationale behind the saying that "the heretic of one generation becomes the orthodox paradigm of the next." This is so because man naturally tends to cling to things as they are rather than risk the uncertainty of the new which, in fact, may be far better. Consequently he opposes any move that appears to be aimed at altering the situation. So much for this digression. We will now turn our attention to the presuppositions of Western Christian orthodox theology and the emergence of new theologies in our day.

Orthodox Christianity has come under increasingly intensive fire since the Renaissance. Historically, theologians have sought to defend the orthodox position against such attacks with varying degrees of success. As we have indicated already, these criticisms of traditional theological inadequacies to meet the needs of modern man can be classified under two broad categories. The first of these holds that the traditional approach is incapable of reconciling the basic Christian message with the new understanding of human existence. Expressed in another way, the failure revolves around the irrelevance of the orthodox theological models as a means of coming to grips with the self-understanding of modern man and his world.

The second category insists that as long as traditional orthodox Christianity uncritically identifies itself with the *status quo* its self-understanding will remain so distorted that it can no more be sensitive to the activity of God in history. The result is that the Church becomes, perhaps unconsciously or sometimes consciously, the agent of the oppressor whose ideologies it espouses in its theologizing.

THE REVISIONIST CRITICISM

In considering the first category of criticism we shall approach it from the perspective of a modified version of David Tracy's* analysis as a springboard. It is not within the scope of the present work to provide a detailed critique of Tracy's discussion. Rather, our purpose is to pave the way for a new approach to Christian theology in Africa. The references to other people's reactions to the traditional theological approach will underline the fact that such a need is universal and constant. To this theology must be responsive if it is to be relevant.

Tracy begins his analysis of the dilemma of the orthodox formulations of the Christian faith with a brief review of the historical circumstances that created the problem. The process that culminates in the present impasse has its genesis in what Tracy calls "the forces for demystifications of the Western religious worldview [which] were set loose by the Enlightenment's demand for freedom from oppressive authorities and freedom for autonomous critical, rational thought."[1] Although the question raised by the Enlightenment was originally aimed at intellectual knowledge, it soon came to be applied to all areas of human cognition including religion. The end result of the initial question was a birth of a new mode of rational analysis which took nothing for granted but demanded that every claim to knowledge justify its *raison d'etre* only on the basis of critical rationality. This, at once, raised for the Church and its theology the problem of validating its cognitive claims. The question which faced the Church was: Can the Church submit its claims to truth to the same rational analysis as other disciplines must? As Tracy expresses it, the question for the Church was:

> Could that mode of rational analysis, itself initially fostered by the basic Christian vision of the world, become the occasion for a process that would both eliminate the merely mystifying components of that vision and yet restore with contemporary integrity Christianity's central vision of God and humanity?[2]

With that question before the Church, the stage was set for the emergence of Christian theologies of various labels. Thus "the struggle

*David Tracy is associate Professor of Philosophical Theology at the University of Chicago Divinity School. He is one of the modern theologians who are attempting to bring order into the confused theological scene of the latter half of the twentieth century. In his book, *Blessed Rage for Order*, Tracy proposes what he calls a Revisionist approach to Christian theology. Highlights of this approach are given here.

of modern theology has been largely the struggle to see how and in what fashion that latter claim can be upheld,"[3] namely, "to restore with contemporary integrity Christianity's central vision of God and humanity."[4]

In grappling with the epistemological problem generated by the above dilemma there have emerged three well known theological models referred to as Orthodox, Liberal and Neo-orthodox, and two recent ones, the Radical and Revisionist theological models. The last model is a brand new one propounded by David Tracy in the book under review. For our purpose here we will examine orthodox and liberal theological models as well as the revisionist model. We will leave out Neo-orthodoxy and the short-lived Radical theologies. This is because Neo-orthodoxy was a reaction against Liberal theology as Radical theology was a reaction against Neo-orthodoxy. The Revisionist model will be treated only in outline form to show it as a new effort to correct the weakness of all the previous attempts in order to restore Christianity's central vision of God.

The main task of each of the traditional theological models to be analyzed is the interpretation of two basic phenomena. These phenomena are the Christian tradition and the contemporary under-standings of human existence.[5] This is to be done in the light of the new cognitive mode necessitated by the Renaissance's insistence that rational analysis is the only passport to cognitive validity. Tracy is convinced that for a theologian committed to executing this task of interpretation, theology must be understood as "a philosophical reflection upon the meanings present in common human experience and language, and upon the meanings present in the Christian fact."[6] In carrying out this reflection the theologian, as it were, moves between two poles which Tracy calls "self referent" and "object referent" poles. The former represents the theologian as a believer and his human experience, while the latter stands for the Christian message as formulated in his traditional confession. It is within these two poles that theologians seek to interpret the phenomena. It will be shown that orthodox theologians failed to come to firm grips with this under-standing in their attempt to meet the challenge.

Orthodox theological model

Modernity demands that the theologian interpret the Christian message in the light of the contemporary self-understanding of human existence. As a rule the orthodox theologian, however, has ignored the reality of the new understanding of human existence. In other words, the theologian operates on the assumption that the claims to a new mode of self-understanding are false. In addition to that assumption, and because of it, the theologian presupposes that the answer to the question raised lies in a "firm commitment to the perennial truths of traditional Christianity.... [This he sees as the] best bulwark against the onslaughts of modern criticism."[7] Of course, by the "perennial truths of traditional Christianity," the theologian means his confessional version of those Christian truths!

On the basis of these presuppositions, the theologian interprets the task of theology as that of discovering new analogies by means of which the "perennial traditional truths" may be explained to the modern man. That is valid as far as it goes, but the tragedy is that it leaves out the second half of the original question, namely, making the Christian message relevant and existentially meaningful in the light of the contemporary new self-understanding. He leaves this out because he has decided *a priori* that the claim to a new mode of viewing human existence does not arise. With that assumption the orthodox theologian proceeds to: "(1) find analogies in nature for these beliefs; (2) use these analogies to provide a systematic understanding of the interconnection of the major mysteries of faith (Christ, Grace, Trinity); and (3) try to relate that analogous understanding to the final end of man (Beatific Vision)."[8]

The weakness of this approach is that the man who asks for help is left out in the cold. He is told in so many words that his problem does not exist in reality but only in his imagination. In consequence, he is told that if he clearly understands the Christian message he will soon discover, to his surprise, that his question does not arise. To proceed this way is to deny that modern man's problem is real, and that it stems from a radical new approach to knowledge fostered by the rise of natural science. This new world view, as already indicated, demands that knowledge is only genuine if it is arrived at through critical empirico-rational analysis. Under this presupposition a mere restatement of Christian doctrines does not touch contemporary man's basic difficulty. Something must be done to grapple with his presuppositions before you can reinterpret the doctrines, otherwise he can not hear what the theologian is saying as long as the two are not operating on the same wave length. By refusing to acknowledge this fact the orthodox theologian fails to address himself to the real issue raised by contemporary man.

Liberal theological model

Unlike the orthodox theologian, the liberal theologian takes modern man's claim to a new self-understanding seriously. In fact, he takes it too seriously and in consequence is committed without without reservation to modern man's values and his stipulation that outside empirico-rational investigation there is no meaningful statement. At the same time, the liberal theologian wants to remain committed to the basic Christian truths and to commend them to modern man.

The problem of the liberal theologian in this circumstance is how to maintain both commitments without sacrificing one for the other. This has never been easy. Given the circumstance, from the outset the liberal theologian's uncritical commitment to the empirico-scientific model as the only viable route to knowledge forced him to reinterpret Christianity. This was done in such a way that those elements in Christianity which are not amenable to the new presuppositions of truth-validity were reinterpreted. This procedure was amply demonstrated in the liberal theologies of Schleiermacher and Ritchl. Schleiermacher, for instance, located religion in human feeling. For him, sin was not a radical evil but ignorance which would eventually be eliminated by proper educational nurture. Schleiermacher opted for this interpretation because the categories of soul and sin have no place in the empirico-scientific model. For Ritchl, religion was seen in terms of morality. Jesus Christ came to demonstrate an ideal moral man could be and he died for what he believed, thus leaving us an example to follow. Like Schleiermacher, Ritchl had to find empirico-scientific categories for expressing Christianity. These he found in morality and moral example.

By restating the fundamental Christian doctrines this way, the liberal theologians sought to avoid meeting head-on the vexing problem of modern man's criteria for validating cognitive claims. If religion is located in human feelings and if Jesus Christ was only our moral example, then claims of divine reality become nothing more than a metaphorical way of expressing psychological phenomena. Religious language in full-blown later liberalism became emotive language that did not refer to any reality other than one's intention to behave in a certain way or to express his approval or disapproval of certain actions. This approach, in a sense, circumvented the demand for empirical verification since Christianity as it was reinterpreted had no objective referent outside of the speaker.

In the end the liberal theologian becomes an anthropologist/

psychologist in the guise of a theologian. His strength lies in his ability to take modern man seriously and, in response, to attempt to see the world through that perspective. His weakness lies in his failure to be critical of the claim of modern man which leads him to reduce all other dimensions of human existence to the empirical level. He ignores the balanced view that man is both physical and spiritual. Man is the link between the physical and the metaphysical and he is not complete unless the two levels of his existence are kept in balance. Man transcends the natural order and he knows this in his self-transcendence, and yet realizes that the very core of his being is immersed in the natural order. In it he moves and has his being but it is not the sum total of his being. This tension must be kept and any attempt to reduce man to any one of these levels or to ignore any of them misses the mark and does not treat man as he is in real life. This was the failure of the liberal theologian.

In summary, our examination of the traditional orthodox Christian theology under the first category of criticism reveals that it fails because it ignores the problem to which it ostensibly seeks to address itself. In the end it becomes unable to relate the meanings present in the Christian message to the meanings present in the human experience and language. Thus the liberal theology which sets out to overcome the dilemma of orthodox theology falls by the wayside. This happens because the liberal theologian uncritically accepted the meanings present in the contemporary human existence and language on their face value as interpreted by contemporary man. Having taken that fatal step he felt obligated to reduce the meanings present in the Christian message to such a form as is consistent with the new mode of human existence. In the process it finds itself unable to perceive the deeper spiritual meanings present in the Christian message for which modern man, deep down in his heart, yearns. In each case it turns out that the only victim of the faulty presupposition is modern man who is in need of the existential salvation or wholeness which eludes him.

Revisionist theological model

It is against this background that the Revisionist theologian has proposed five presuppositions which he calls five theses. These, he argues, should form the basis for developing a Christian theology that can be faithful to the central Christian vision of God and yet be relevant and responsive to modern man's self-understanding of his existence. Each of these theses will now be stated in outline form.

They are:

1. The two principal sources for theology are Christian texts and common human experience and language.[9]

Here, Tracy insists that the Christian message must be shown to be adequate for meeting the existential needs of man. But if the theologian is to be successful in showing this he must first seek to analyze both human experience and language, and the Christian message as formulated. Without such analysis the theologian can neither grasp the intrinsic meanings nor categories that will enable man in his new mode of understanding to appropriate those meanings. The procedure that is being suggested here is not a gratuitous one but one that is demanded by the very nature of the claim of the Christian message. As Tracy puts it:

> This commitment to determine methods and criteria which can show the adequacy of Christian self-understanding for all human experience is a task demanded by the very logic of the Christian affirmation; more precisely, by the Christian claim to provide the authentic way to understand our common human existence.[10]

The task of theology, so understood, rules out the inadequate methodology of the orthodox theologian which sets out to disregard the claims of modern man to an altered mode of self-understanding. Consequently he operated under the assumption that what modern man really needed is a new analogy for interpreting the Gospel. In the place of this, the Revisionist contends that the theologian must operate on the assumption that the task of theology involves a commitment to investigate critically both the Christian faith in its several expressions and the contemporary experience in its several cultural expressions.[11]

2. The theological task will involve a critical correlation of the results of the investigations of the two sources of theology.[12]

While acknowledging his indebtedness to Tillich for the concept of correlation, Tracy maintains that Tillich was inconsistent in executing the task of correlation. He points out that Tillich does not call for a critical correlation of the results of one's investigations of the situation and the message. Rather, his method affirms the need for a correlation of the questions expressed in the situation with the answers provided by the Christian message. [13] That this is Tillich's position is underlined in his adoption of existentialist philosophy as the only viable stance from which his correlation can be effected. A commitment to a critical investigation does not allow one to tie one's self to the apronstring of any one critical system. For if the situation is to be taken with full seriousness, then its answers to its own questions must also be investigated critically. [14] To do this successfully compels one to employ all available critical tools if one is to be satisfied that both the situation and the answers have been investigated from all angles and in all their ramifications.

3. **The principal method of investigation of the source common to human experience and language can be described as a phenomenology of religious dimension present in everyday and scientific experience and language.** [15]

This thesis presupposes that all human experiences, no matter what area is involved, ultimately reveal dimensions that can legitimately be described as religious. Inasmuch as the Christian message asserts that it has universal existential relevance, the role of the theologian, therefore, is to show how and why the existential meanings proper to Christian self-understanding are present in the common human experience. [16] It must be noted that the term experience is here not limited to sense-data but is applied to all areas of human consciousness and all that humanness entails.

Tracy makes it clear that he does not want to leave the impression that the phenomenological method is the only viable one for the enterprise. He, however, feels that "a recognition of the real possibilities of that method promises a new surety to the several attempts to explicate the religious dimension of our common experience and language." [17] In any case, whichever analytic tool is adopted, the aim is to explicate those characteristics of our shared human experience which are unamenable to explanations other than religious. The presence of such characteristics and the universal nature of the Christian claim necessitates that this effort be made.

4. The principal method of investigation of the source, the Christian tradition, can be described as an historical and hermeneutical investigation of classical Christian texts.[18]

By means of the historical method the theologian initially seeks to reconstruct the historical milieu in which the basic texts of Christian self-understanding are hammered out. As important as this reconstruction is, it is not enough. In addition, he must find a hermeneutic method capable of discovering, *at least*, the central meanings of the principal textual expressions of Christianity (viz; the Scriptural).[19]

The historical and hermeneutical investigations must complement each other because while the former can determine the historical context and the 'linguistic structure of the images and symbols involved in the text... the meaning of major import *to the theologian* remains a concern that can be formulated by a question like the following: what is the mode-of-being-in-the-world referred to by the text? This question is not answered until an explicitly hermeneutic enterprise is advanced.''[20] In other words, there is a difference between the literal and the referent import of a text and it is only by a combination of the historical and hermeneutical methods that the theologian can discern the referent meanings.

5. To determine the truth-status of the results of one's investigations into the meaning of both common human experience and Christian texts the theologian should employ an explicitly transcendental or metaphysical mode of reflection.[21]

This fifth thesis is the logical implication from the first four theses. For, after critical investigation of the two sources of theology, the meanings present in both human experience and Christian texts, the time comes to test the truth status of the results if our intended correlation is to be worthwhile. To achieve this objective requires the evolution of an appropriate mode of reflection that will be able to determine their significant similarities and differences and their truth-value[22] before correlating them.

This, Tracy concedes, is difficult to find and defend to everyone's satisfaction. The difficulty inheres in the nature of the problem itself. Whatever mode of reflection one adopts, it must be capable of articulating both conceptual and symbolic categories of reflection. This means that it must be comprehensive enough to deal with all categories of human knowledge, be it on physical or spiritual levels. Tracy is convinced that one clear way of articulating the nature of the reflective discipline capable of such inquiry is to describe it as transcendental in its modern formulation or metaphysical in its more traditional expression.[23] This is predicated on the assumption that if all human experiences have religious dimensions, as these theses presuppose, then the more common empirical mode of reflection as such cannot account for all areas of human experience without tending towards reductionism. This cries out for a transcendental mode of reflection as this is the only one comprehensive enough to cover all areas of human experience.

Aware of the many unfortunate connotations which the term metaphysics arouses, Tracy is quick to distinguish its use here from the traditional and neo-traditional usages. He points out that metaphysics is not a deductive mode of reflection; it is not inductive nor yet a conceptual poetry. He declares:

> Metaphysics is neither axiomatic nor inductive argumentation. Rather, its mode of argument can be more properly described as transcendental in the exact sense that metaphysical argument shows that certain basic beliefs must necessarily be maintained as basic conditions of the possibility of our understanding of existing at all.[24]

If that assumption is accepted, then it is only reasonable to conclude that by its nature the metaphysical mode of reflection is comprehensive enough to serve as the criterion for analyzing the truth-status of the cognitive claims of all areas of human experience.

These five theses are developed and validated by Tracy in the book under review. As we have indicated earlier, it is not our purpose to go into any detail here. What concerns us is to point out that unlike the liberal theologian, the revisionist insists that the empirical-criteria stipulation for meaningfulness by the modern man is not viable. In its place the revisionist is proposing the transcendental mode of reflection. This mode is seen as the only viable comprehensive mode of reflection that can be the medium by means of which the common human experience and its basic religious dimensions on the one hand, and the central Christian vision of God on the other, can be analyzed, validated and correlated. Thus the revisionist model makes room for taking modern man's self-understanding seriously but not uncritically. It makes provision for analyzing his experience and language in order to lead him to see that the inherent religious dimensions cannot adequately be accounted for within the empirical language. The transcendental language, the revisionist argues, is capable of both analyzing the meanings present in the shared experience and the Christian message as well as correlating them.

LIBERATION THEOLOGIANS' CRITICISM

The second ground on which orthodox Christian theology has been criticized as inadequate is its virtual indentification with the *status quo* or the prevailing cultural ethos. Such an identification not only distorts its theological vision but it also deadens its sensitivity to the presence of God in history. This is the criticism which the liberation theologians have levelled against orthodox theology. Liberation theologians' views range from moderate to radical proportions. They are, however, agreed on certain basics. They are agreed that orthodox Christian theology is impotent in the face of economic and political oppression because it is vitiated by the imposed ideology of the ruling class. In light of this, they insist that theology must be liberated from its ideological captivity before it can see its mission clearly. In the discussion that follows we shall present Juan Luis Segundo's criticisms of orthodox theological presuppositions to represent the views of liberation theologians.*

Liberation theologians contend that the dominant ideology in a given age comes from the ruling class which invents and maintains the ideology at all costs in order to keep things as they are. By this, they mean that the thought-patterns as well as the perceptions of any age are determined by the prevailing ideology which owes its existence to the powers-that-be. This means that even the theologians are not

*Juan Luis Segundo, S. J., is a Roman Catholic priest/scholar from Latin America. He studied in France, earning his Doctorate of Letters from the University of Paris. He serves as the director of the Peter Faber Pastoral Centre in Montevideo, his native home.

Segundo is one of the leading liberation theologians from Latin America. He has several books and articles to his credit. His *The Liberation of Theology* which grew out of his series of lectures while serving as Visiting Professor at Harvard Divinity School, is analyzed here.

exempt from the pervasive influence of such ideology. They point out that historically, it was after Emperor Constantine made Christianity the official religion of the Roman Empire that Christianity gradually lost its prophetic dynamism. This came to be replaced by acquiesence and apathy, contrary to its original transforming mission in the world. To that extent, they argue:

> Every theology is political, even one that does not speak or think in political terms. The influence of politics on theology and every other cultural sphere cannot be evaded any more than the influence of theology on politics and other spheres of human thinking. [25]

The influence of this reigning ideology is so subtle that the Church and its theologians may not be aware of it. However, any objective analysis of the major presuppositions of any theology will reveal such influence.

The presuppositions of orthodox theology which bear the marks of the hidden influence of the *status quo* may be summarized as follows. The most basic of these from which other presuppositions are derived is the unbalanced stress on personal salvation and its emphasis on the next world. Such a stress tends to divert attention from the inequalities and injustices of this world to a pie in the sky where all wrongs will be righted and the faithful accorded their appropriate reward. It was this type of theology that led Karl Marx to dismiss religion as the opiate of the people. In the opinion of the liberation theologians such a view of religion is a distortion of the biblical message which shows clearly that God is concerned with man's well-being not only in the next world but also *here* and *now*. The Exodus experience, the prophetic teachings as represented by Isaiah, Amos and Micah, as well as the teachings of Jesus Christ, especially as contained in his inaugural sermon in Luke, chapter 4, are cited as evidence of God's concern for man's condition *here* and *now*. They maintain that the orthodox theologian's usual tendency to interpret Jesus' declaration in Luke, chapter 4, in terms of spiritual liberation *alone* betrays their subservience to the ruling class whose agents they are, perhaps unwittingly.

The same presupposition is the underlying basis of the theologian's theory of two orders – the supernatural and the natural – of responsibility. The theologian's unconscious desire to assuage his conscience for failing to bring divine judgment to bear on the injustice in society leads him to see the Church's sole responsibility as preparing souls for heaven (the supernatural order). Consequently, existence on the natural order is seen as the responsibility of Caesar. Such a view is forcefully illustrated in the following Eastern Orthodox expression of its self-understanding. As far as the Eastern Orthodox Church prior to the communist revolution was concerned:

> Its task in relation to the world is to penetrate it from within. The world is transformed by the sacramental activities of the Church. It is not the task of the Church to interfere with social life or with politics, but the more it draws its members into its sacramental communion the more will its influence be felt in the world. [26]

In defense of such a culturally imposed self-understanding, orthodox theology, having seen itself to be above politics, attacks any theologian who dares to suggest that theology must be related to the whole of life, including politics. Liberation theologians' reactions to this is that "when academic theology accuses liberation theology of being political and engaging in politics, thus ignoring its own tie-up with the political status quo, it is really looking for a scapegoat to squelch its own guilt complex."[27]

Another presupposition of orthodox theology is the assertion that theology is universal and colour blind, hence status-blind. It is easy for a traditional theologian who begins with this assumption to respond to the conditions of Blacks in the U.S. or South Africa by erecting what Segundo aptly calls "an ideological edifice in which the *cause* of the oppressed people's suffering is not even mentioned, much less studied. In this way, law, philosophy, and religion, join with the mechanism of oppression and become its witting or unwitting accomplices."[28] The logic here is clear. If theology is colour blind or status blind, then the theologian can theologize on freedom in spiritual and general terms without any reference to a concrete people in a concrete historical context who are suffering from political and economic oppression before his eyes. The theologian does this unaware of the ideological undercurrent that conditioned his interpretation of the Scriptures.

The third presupposition of orthodox theology which renders its theologizing irrelevant, and which has its roots in cultural conditioning, is its understanding of eschatology. For traditional theology, eschatology is an event which only God will usher into history without any human participation. In other words, all man has to do is endure whatever deprivation his society metes out to him with the hope that in God's good time the *eschaton* will arrive and his tears will be wiped dry. In the meantime, the oppressors continue to wax strong and enjoy the goods of the world with abandon. For the liberation theologian, this concept of eschatology is defective and is a product of a subtle desire on the part of the theologian not to upset the apple cart. It is a device to ensure that the social structure remains intact because any suggestions that God expects man to participate in ushering in the *eschaton* entails a change in the social structure. Any meaningful process of humanization in an oppressive society must involve a change in the political and economic set up. In order to forestall any such change traditional theology, under the influence of the prevailing ideology, ostensibly hides behind the facade that only God, without human involvement, can bring about the *eschaton*. In the interim period things can remain as they have always been!

The point at issue in the criticism levelled by the liberation theologians against the faulty presuppositions of orthodox theology is not that the latter has no biblical support for its views. The point is to reveal the fact that all theologies are contextually conditioned. For the choice of the sections of the Bible for interpretation and the hermeneutical principles adopted are all subject to the subtle demands of the underlying covert or overt presuppositions. The danger lies in the theologian's failure to realize this or in his desire to conceal this knowledge and thereby pretend to theologize objectively as led by God's Spirit. No theologian can even become sensitive to the promptings of God's Spirit until he consciously acknowledges his presuppositions and is willing to deal with them under the searchlight of God. Without this it is a farce for a theologian to talk of divine leadership in his theological reflection on the Bible.

Liberation theologians, like the orthodox theologians, regard the Bible as the fountainhead of theology and, therefore, the Bible remains the point of contact between all theologians. This is consistent with what Segundo calls the pedagogical function of the Scriptures. As the Word of God, the past and the present are simultaneously present in the Bible. This is an essential hermeneutical principle which presupposes that God reveals the various aspects of his nature to people in different situations in response to their peculiar needs in those circumstances. This underscores the need to take context into consideration. When this is done the record of God's self-disclosure in the past becomes the occasion for a new disclosure in a new historical situation which can be discerned by those who are spiritually sensitive. This is the meaning of the pedagogical function of the Scriptures. Thus the theologian who operates on this principle has a tremendous responsibility not only to be open to what God may reveal, but also to be prepared to consider what he may decipher from the revelatory signals even if they be contrary to his previous conceptions. We limit ourselves from perceiving divine revelatory activity in all of its inexaustible richness if we refuse to acknowledge the reality of contextual conditioning of our theological perception.

The liberation theologians are convinced that these presuppositions, which render orthodox theology ineffective because its theological perception is distorted, are deep-seated. That being so, the time has come for a painful, radical surgical operation on its methodology. Without a new methodology which is consciously developed and accepted in the light of the concrete historical context, the liberation theologians fear that theology will continue to be unresponsive to human conditions. In light of this, Segundo has proposed a new methodoloy which he calls the hermeneutical circle. He defines this as "the continuing change in our interpretation of the Bible which is dictated by the continuing change in our present day reality both individual and societal"[29]

Segundo argues that only a strict adherence to the new hermeneutical circle as a methodology can guarantee that the theologian will be able to "relate the past and the present in dealing with the Word of God."[30] He sees this as the only cure for the "naive belief that the Word of God is applied to human realities inside some antiseptic laboratory that is totally immune to the ideological tendencies and struggles of the present day."[31]

Having now laid bare what the liberation theologians consider to be the weakness and the cause of the inadequacies of orthodox theology, Segundo proceeds to enunciate four decisive factors for the successful operation of his hermeneutical circle. They are:

> Firstly, there is our way of experiencing reality which leads us to ideological suspicion.

> Secondly, there is the application of our ideological suspicion to the whole ideological superstructure in general and to theology in particular.

> Thirdly, there comes a new way of experiencing theological reality that leads us to exegetical suspicion, that is, to the

suspicion that the prevailing interpretation of the Bible has not taken important pieces of data into account.

Fourthly, we have our new hermeneutic, that is, our way of interpreting the fountainhead of our faith (i.e. Scripture) with the new elements at our disposal.[32]

These presuppositions, as far as Segundo is concerned, constitute the canon against which the success and failure of any liberation theologizing must be evaluated. It is not our intention to determine whether or not the hermeneutical circle as outlined here can be faithful to the pedagogical function of the Bible in theologizing. What is certain (and that is our interest in the movement) is that Segundo has not only called attention to underlying reasons for the inadequacy of orthodox theology, but has also proposed a lucid procedure that enables him to avoid the pitfalls of orthodox theology.

SOME LESSONS

Now that we have examined the two categories of criticism of orthodox theology which have led to the emergence of new theologies, it is apropos at this juncture to draw some lessons. We must begin by asserting the obvious – that there is no such thing as a presupposition-less theology. In his attempt to discern the meanings present in both the Christian faith and the common human experience and to relate them to human needs, the theologian must be aware of the cultural influences that shape him and equip him with his conceptual tools. Unless this is realized by the theologian, his theology is likely to become tied to the past and, consequently, insensitive to the present working of God. For he is still at work just as he was in the past, to make his will known. In view of this perennial danger, and consistent with the preceding criticism of orthodox theology, the theologian must take seriously the following three factors.

Firstly, the theologian must consciously accept the fact that all theologies are contextually conditioned. This being so, he must not take his inherited formulation of the Christian faith as sacrosanct dogmas that may not be modified or even jettisoned if need be.

Secondly, he must realize that the Christian faith *qua* Christian faith is such that no one can exhaust its meaning. While it is always expressed in different contexts, it can never be exhausted nor exhaustively understood by the interpretive filter of one context.[33]

Thirdly, the theologian must take the context of his audience seriously, and, using all available appropriate investigative tools, analyze it critically. In doing this he must remain radically open to the possibilities which that context may offer for a new perception of human self-understanding. This open state of mind will enable the theologian to perceive the new meanings which such a mode-of-being in the world may generate in the process of his effort to relate the faith to their needs within that context. The result is that theological understanding and its formulation will be enriched in a way that would have been impossible without the new context.

If the theologian is to be able to proceed successfully along the suggested lines and to avoid the mistakes of orthodox theologians he needs to avail himself of all the critical tools necessary, not only to understand the Bible but also his world view and the self-understanding entailed herein. This is what Van Harvey means when he says:

> Theology, therefore, requires the acquisition and development of the sociological imagination, that is, a quality of mind and reflection that enables its possessor to understand the larger historical scene in terms of its meaning for the inner life and the external career of a variety of the individuals.[34]

Such an understanding is essential if the theologian is to accomplish the theological task in the modern world. That task, in the words of David Tracy, is "the dramatic confrontation, the mutual illuminations and corrections, the possible basic reconciliation between the principal values, cognitive claims, and existential faiths of both a re-interpreted post-modern consciousness and a re-interpreted Christianity."[35]

What we have attempted to do in this chapter is to argue that the presuppositions of traditional Western Christian theology have prevented it from being relevant for man in this modern age. The new theologies which we examined in this chapter emerged as a protest against the insensitivity of that theology to the realities of the new era in which it is called upon to justify its claims to relevancy. In summary, the criticisms levelled against traditional Western Christian theology hinge on two poles. First, it hinges on its inability to reconcile the basic

Christian message with the new understanding of human existence. This is so for two reasons: While orthodox theology refuses to accept the reality of a new mode of self-understanding, liberal theology swallowed the claim to a new mode of self-understanding hook, line and sinker. Consequently, liberal theology jettisons those eternal elements in the Christian message that cannot be forced into the categories of scientism.

The second pole, as seen by the liberation theologians, is the uncritical identification with the *status quo* of traditional Western Christian theology. This identification makes theology function as the agent of the power structure dedicated, sometimes inadvertently, to the preservation of the *status quo* at the expense of the oppressed. It is argued that as long as this is the case, theology remains irrelevant since it becomes insensitive to the divine liberating activity in human history.

In addition to the above defects of traditional Western Christian theology, this writer identifies another one of its presuppositions that makes it an inadequate vehicle of the Christian faith to Africa. The defect is the quasi-scientific world view which shaped the formulation of that theology. That this is the case will be shown in chapter three which compares and contrasts the quasi-scientific and African world views.

3

QUASI-SCIENTIFIC WORLD VIEW VERSUS AFRICAN WORLD VIEW

In the preceding chapter we examined certain of the presuppositions of orthodox Christian theology as expressed by its interaction with other cultures/sub-cultures of the world. This was done in order to isolate the reasons which, its critics say, contribute to its inadequacy to meet the needs of contemporary man in a way that justifies Christianity's claim to authentic relevance for the vital needs of the total man.

One group of critics, if you will recall, points out that the failure of traditional theology lies in its inability to take contemporary man's new mode of self-understanding seriously enough to warrant a critical examination of it. It contends that having failed to do this, traditional theology finds it impossible to evolve new ways of relating the needs of contemporary man to the Christian message. The other group blames the irrelevance of traditional theology on its unconscious indentification with the *status quo* whose ideology has conditioned the theological perception of the traditional theologian. These summaries of the findings of the critics may be reduced to one statement: Traditional theology fails to take fully into account the new context within which it is called upon to discern divine revelation. This failure is due mostly to an unconscious *inability to come to grips with the stark reality that theologizing is never done in a cultural vacuum.* As a result of this lapse, the traditional theologian loses sight of the fact that the *Word*, as it were, must always become *flesh* in each concrete situation if people are to "behold his glory as the glory of the only begotten Son of God" (John 1:14). On the basis of its particular diagnosis of orthodox theology, each group of critics proposes a new methodology for theologizing aimed at remedying the dereliction of orthodox theology.

As indicated earlier, the rationale behind the presentation of the views of these theologians is to show that orthodox theology has been criticized for being inadequate not only in meeting the spiritual needs of Africans, the primary concern of this book, but also in meeting human needs elsewhere. The latter has been amply demonstrated to be the case, as disclosed in the analysis of the revisionist and liberation theologians. The time has come for us to present our case for the ineffectiveness of the traditional Christian theological presuppositions in Africa. Our thesis is that traditional Christian theology has been ineffective in Africa because it is conditioned by a quasi-scientific world view which blinds it to, and thereby makes it unresponsive to, the reality of the African's self-understanding within his own world view.

In order to substantiate this thesis we will delineate both the quasi-scientific world view of the Western Christian theologian and the world view with its attendant traditional religious practices that characterizes much of Africa. It will then be shown that any theologizing from such a quasi-scientific world view is bound to deny or, at best, to ignore the African world view and thereby renders the resultant theology irrelevant to the existential needs of the African. This will prepare the ground for a proposal of new guidelines for Christian theology in the African context. These guidelines will be the theme of the next chapter.

THE QUASI-SCIENTIFIC WORLD VIEW OF THE NINETEENTH CENTURY CHRISTIAN THEOLOGIAN

Kenneth S. Latourette says that prior to the eighteen hundreds the Christian Church was convinced, rightly or wrongly, that African traditional religion "would succumb before an energetic approach by a more highly organized religion whether it were Christianity or Islam."[1] For some unknown reasons, observes Latourette, "before AD 1800 that type of approach was not made."[2] To be sure, Christianity was introduced to the coastal fringes of sub-Saharan Africa towards the end of the fifteenth century, mostly by the Portuguese Roman Catholics. This initial planting of Christianity, however, did not survive for long, for, "with the decay of Portuguese power in the seventeenth and eighteenth centuries it...dwindled. In some areas it has disappeared [by the nineteenth century]."[3]

It is, therefore, generally accepted that Christianity was not effectively introduced to Black Africa until the fourth decade of the nineteenth century. By that time the biblical world view of the Christian faith had been eroded in Europe by successive waves of historical, scientific and philosophical ferment. A vital biblical world view is predicated on the acceptance of interaction between man and spiritual forces of both evil and good. Prior to and including the medieval period when Christianity came into its own in Europe, there was no serious problem in accepting the reality of the spiritual realm. Visions of angels, other spiritual beings, demon possession, witches and wizards were commonplace topics of conversation. Church teachings and practices reinforced the belief in the reality of the involvement of spiritual forces in human affairs.

Under such an atmosphere it was easy to sense the presence of God in nature and to symbolize that presence in the use of material elements which were regarded as concrete tokens of his presence. The doctrine of the incarnation itself is the early Church's affirmation of the reality of divine interaction with man in history. As Miller puts it, the doctrine of incarnation was to affirm that "once more he [God] walked among men as he had before the fall when history had not yet begun. Christ was the mediator joining a fallen world and a distant God."[4] This awareness of the presence of God in his world was further vivified in the Church by means of such symbols as the Eucharist which, for the medieval Church, was a daily enactment of the truth of the incarnation.

With the dawn of the Renaissance and the subsequent industrialization and technological breakthroughs, changes set in which eventually transformed nature. Consequently man gradually lost contact with those aspects of nature which reminded him of God and man's dependence on him. The Reformation did not help the situation; rather it aggravated it by rejecting the religious symbolisms which were once used to represent divine immanence sacramentally. For instance, in the hands of Calvin and Zwingli, the Eucharist no longer represented a sharing in the immediate presence of Christ,[5] but became "mere signs commemorating the historical facts that Christ was long ago present on this earth."[6] "Thus the God within nature as represented by the bread and the transcended God as symbolized by the ascension of Christ came to be separated from each other."[7] The result was that at the dawning of the age of Enlightenment the view was held that God "has become a *Deus Absconditus*, hidden somewhere behind the silence of infinite space, and our literary symbols can only make the most distant allusions to him or to the natural world which used to be his abiding place and home."[8] The Newtonian mechanical view of the universe further accentuated the growing feeling that interaction between the spiritual realm, if indeed it exists, and the material universe is superfluous. As a machine, the universe once set in motion can go on eternally without any further intervention from its Cosmic Engineer.

Faced with the concept of an absent God in a world that is no longer regarded as the arena of the spiritual-human encounter, the theological arm of the Enlightenment responded with the development of a deistic theology. Deistic theology was a rational theology that does not require that there be immediate interaction between man and the spiritual forces immanent on the earth. The doctrine of the incarnation was not seen by deists as a necessity, for a special revelation is not essential to deism. Besides, the traditional place of the Bible as the inspired witness to God's activities in history was relegated to the background. For the eighteenth century theologians God could only be inferred from the existence of the world on the basis of *causal analogy*. By causal analogy they implied that just as you can infer an intelligent purposeful agent behind any work of art, for example, so you can postulate divine intelligence behind nature. In view of this, the Bible was seen as superfluous; hence the biblical world view and the theology fostered by it could be discarded without any loss.

The Christian faith was then summarized in five basic beliefs which, as the enlightened man claimed, could only befit the dignity of rational men everywhere. These were the ideas of creation, God the Creator, freedom, immortality of the soul, and reward or punishment after death. Other than these, such traditional Christian beliefs as the incarnation, divine activities in the world, as well as spiritual forces in general believed to be immanent on the earth, were considered obsolete in a world which had come of age. In fact, they were viewed as tantamount to an "illusion born of ignorance and perpetrated by the priest in order to accentuate the fears of mankind and so hold it in subjection."[9] In the place of such an illusion the "enlightened man" created a rational religion whose open book of revelation was *nature*. God, they claimed, was revealed in *nature* for any rational man to apprehend; hence there was no need for any Scripture purporting to be a book of revelation.[10]

The tenuousness of a deistic theology based on such precarious philosophical presuppositions had been exposed with the posthumous publication of Hume's book, *Dialogues Concerning Natural Religion*.

In this book, David Hume debunked the Enlightenment's natural theology which was based on casual analogy. Hume, according to Frederick Ferre, maintained that "the empirical principle of inference depends upon prior observation of casual relations between various kinds of things: e.g. between the kind of thing we call smoke, and the kind of thing we call fire."[11] The point Hume was making was that before the existence of God can be inferred from the fact of the universe, as the deists did, there must be a prior observation of the universe emerging from the activities of a creator-God. In the absence of such an empirical observation, this being the only universe we know, it is logically incorrect to conclude that this universe was the handiwork of a purposive intelligence called God. For Hume, then, on purely logical ground, all such arguments for the existence of God "...are defective; the only constantly invulnerable position is that of a skeptic who treats all with the same even-handed disdain."[12] Hume, therefore, called for "a total suspension of judgment," which, he said, "is here our only reasonable recourse."[13]

On logical grounds Hume, in essence, has raised a serious question not only about the existence of God but the whole concept of the spiritual realm. This not only shattered the self-confidence of the deist who thought he had circumvented the theological impasse caused by the scientific world view by restoring faith in God through logical argument. It also threw the whole Christian community which accepted his logic into great confusion. This was an existential problem that shocked the Christian community not only intellectually but also emotionally. As Becker describes it, the impact was "nothing less than the intellectual *cause célèbre* of the age and one that stirred the emotions of men.... The reader was concerned to know whether there was a God to care for his immortal soul or no God and no immortal soul to care for."[14]

In response to the problem thus created, Immanuel Kant and George Hegel, each in his own way, struggled intellectually to undo what Hume had done and to restore the Christian understanding of God without the orthodox biblical world view. It is now generally agreed that Kant's success was limited to establishing the concept of God merely as a postulate or an idea needed to uphold moral values. Hegel was even less successful from the standpoint of biblical religion. For Hegel reduced Christianity to philosophy thus robbing "the traditional theisms of its transcendence and the distinction between God and man. Besides this defect, Hegel's system presupposes an eventual elimination of religion when man becomes rational enough to outgrow his need for the religious myths in which religion now clothes the Absolute.''[15]

Other theologians attempted to recapture the ethos of the biblical religion and its world view without success. Like the proverbial Humpty Dumpty, not even all the king's men and all the king's horses could put it together again! It was impossible to regain the lost ground. On the surface, however, the cultural superstructure built on the now dislodged biblical foundation still lingered on. After all, was it not the same culture that gave birth to the Renaissance, science and the Enlightenment? Were not the means of communication the creation of the culture? In the light of this it was "still possible for many years for those in authority to speak of God and his goodness in general terms.... [It must be remembered that] for fifteen hundred years christianity had baptized the European arts, politics, social order and economic outlook in religiosity,"[16] hence it was not easy to notice the hollowness of the "God – talk" that continued for a long time.

It may be argued that many years had elapsed between the peak of deism of the eighteenth century and the missionary movement of the mid-ninteenth century. The former may be said to be mainly a movement of the intellectuals while the latter is considered to be a religiously conservative biblicist reaction. That this may be true to a point is the rationale for describing the resultant world view as quasi-scientific. We must not lose sight of the fact that a century of deistic teaching had left its impact on the society. The religious atmosphere having been tainted by philosophical erosion of the medieval religious hegemony, it was bound to have dilutionary effects on the biblical world view. With regard to the pervading influence of culture on man, the so-called conservative grassroots Christians who led the missionary movement of the mid-nineteenth century were conservative only in relation to the deists. They would be ultra-liberals compared to medieval Christians. It is true that they were pietists and biblical literalists judged by the standard of the intellectual deists, but these must be understood as relative labels far removed from medieval Christianity and the biblical world view.

It cannot be over-emphasized that it is not enough to say that the missionary movement of the mid-nineteenth century was led by religiously conservative, biblical literalists. We must go on to add that these labels used in describing them are to be understood as relative terms within the context of mid-nineteenth century Christianity and not in terms of medieval Christianity which is our point of departure in the argument. Unless our labels are so defined, the impression would be given that a century of deistic teaching and attempted modifications by other intellectuals had no significant influence on the masses whose pace and content of intellectual orientation were set by the intellectuals. If the usual assumption that the average man is a generation behind the intellectual is correct, then we have had more than three generations in this case for the average man to have been significantly affected.

In the light of the above, we conclude that by the time Christianity was introduced into Black Africa in the fourth decade of the nineteenth century the world view of the Christian theologian retained only a veneer of the biblical world view. This conclusion is borne out by the attitude of the missionaries toward African world views. The missionary world view. By virtue of such a reinterpretation of the Bible, Christians view. It is true that we could still talk about God, heaven, angels, Satan, Holy Spirit, evil forces; but these were no more than cultural cliches that lacked the existential dynamism they once had prior to and during the medieval period.

Under an ethos such as this, biblical references to demon possession, angels and spiritual forces operating in the affairs of men could still be mouthed though with diminished emotional overtones. But on the intellectual level the theologian found it necessary to reinterpret them, at best, as symbols without ontic content or, at worst, as the figment of the imagination of a primitive age under the influence of an ancient world view. By virtue of such a reinterpretation of the Bible, Christians could talk of Christ's power to save from sin but not enthusiastically of his power to destroy the works of the Devil and to save, to the utmost, those who are committed to him. For instance, the nineteenth century theologian could still quote Ephesians 6:12, "For we are not fighting against human beings, but against the wicked spiritual forces in the heavenly world, the rulers, authorities, and cosmic powers of this dark age," but not with the same meaning Paul gave them when he penned those lines to the Christians in Ephesus. When Paul wrote that letter the Ephesian world view was the same as the biblical world view and consequently the message had existential significance for both Paul and his audience. The situation was different for the nineteenth century Christian theologian.

This, of course, was not yet the orthodox scientific world view that rejects all such cultural lip service to the existence of the spiritual realm.

The orthodox scientific world view presupposes a closed universe which self-originated, and denies the existence of the spiritual realm. It is this major distinction between the orthodox world view and the one described above that leads us to brand it a quasi-scientific world view. This distinction is useful because it still half-heartedly acknowledged the reality of the spiritual dimension. This acknowledgement, by the standard of the medieval era, can only be described as an afterglow of the biblical world view.

It was against such a distilled biblical world view that Christian theologians came to Africa in the nineteenth century. But the African, as we shall soon see, had a completely different world view from that of the nineteenth century Christian theologian. Given the fact of the cultural influence on one's perception as explained in chapter two, how would the Christian theologian react to the world view typical of much of Africa and the resultant religion? This is the main question we must keep before us as we describe the African's world view and his self-understanding arising from it.

AFRICAN WORLD VIEW AND RELIGION*

This author is very much aware that Africa is a large continent with diverse peoples and culture. In that case no one may be so presumptuous as to claim to describe African religions and world views in the singular. However, in spite of the differences, there is a core of Africanness that runs through their cultures and religions. In view of this one may speak legitimately of an African world view, the local peculiarities notwithstanding. While the writer concedes that his perception of the African world view bears the stamp of the part of Africa he experiences, he is convinced that the rest of Africa is not too far off from his description.

African world view and religion will here be discussed under four concepts. These are concepts of the earth, man, his place on the earth, and his utilization of what he considers to be divinely ordained provisions for coping with the uncertainties of life. There will be no detailed presentation of these, but enough will be said to highlight the

---

*Much of the material in this section is based on chapter four of the author's *Nigerian Traditional Religion: Beliefs and Modes of Coping with Uncertainties of Life*, published by University Press Limited, Ibadan, Nigeria, 1981.

contrast between the quasi-scientific world view of the nineteenth century Christian theologian and the African. The reader is invited to note the contrast as this will be the basis of the argument for new guidelines for theology in Africa which will be presented in chapter four.

The earth

In the African world view the earth is seen as a reality created by God. It is the arena in which man is to live out his life in preparation for a fuller life in heaven. In other words, the earth is not a permanent abode for man; it is a temporary proving ground for heaven. This is why the earth is symbolically referred to as a "farm" to which people go in the morning only to return home in the evening after the day's labour. Another figure that is used to designate the earth is that of a "market" where people buy and sell with the intention of making gain. At the end of the day they return home to count their gains and losses. These metaphors are intended to keep one constantly reminded that his sojourn on earth is temporary, and yet what is done here has eternal consequences. Ultimately, everyone is accountable to God at the end of his term here on earth.

The earth is also believed to have fallen short of God's original intention for it. This fact is described in the various myths of creation and man's alienation from God. The earth bears the brunt of man's disobedience. Consequently, the earth has become the battleground where evil forces are pitted against man. The curse on the earth by reason of man's sin is final. The earth has no chance of ever becoming anything better than it is now. There is no eschatological provision for a transformed earth.

As a reality, the earth is multidimensional. The ordinary man sees only the physical dimension, but there are other dimensions which are not visible to the natural eye. For instance, there is the dimension of the "vital force," variously referred to as "nyama," "psychic force," "energy" or "dynamism." Most scholars seem to prefer the term "dynamism." Smith defines dynamism as "the belief in and the practices associated with the belief in hidden, mysterious, super-sensible, pervading energy, powers, potencies and forces,"[17] which are thought to constitute a dimension of the earth. Dynamism, though neutral, may be tapped for good or ill. This power is accessible to those whose consciousness has been expanded through occult powers. Such people are not only able to become aware of this dimension of the earth, but they can also utilize it for their needs either to help or harm others.

In fact, the dynamism is so real that it is believed that when a *bona fide* "medicine man" goes in search of herbs for his medicine to cure a particular disease, this dynamism directs him to the proper herbs. The belief here is that dynamism is capable of incarnating herbs for the purpose of helping the herbalist to gain therapeutic success with his herbal preparations.

Witches and wizards that haunt and harass people also owe their occult powers to this dimension of the earth. By virtue of their utilization of this "force," witches and wizards can become visible as well as turn themselves into any form of life at will in pursuit of their nefarious activities. The concept of magic also owes its origin to this dimension.[18]

There is another dimension of the earth inhabited by spirits and ghosts. This dimension, like that of dynamism, is also invisible to the naked or uninitiated eye. These malevolent spirits and ghosts may be enlisted in the services of the men of the occult. The spirits and ghosts are, however, not all-powerful; hence man can be protected against their machination. The means of protection can be obtained at a cost from "medicine men." The "medicine man" in turn obtains such means through ritual manipulation of the "vital force," or dynamism, which we have already discussed.

In addition to such magical help, the ancestral spirits can also offer protection against the evil spirits and ghosts. Ancestral spirits and divinities, while resident in the spirit-world, are also immanent in a dimension of the earth which is perhaps distinct from the two already mentioned. This is a bit fuzzy, but in any case you have here on earth with a hierarchy of dimensions – the physical, the "dynamism" or "vital force," the evil spirits and ghosts, and perhaps the station from which the immanent ancestral spirits and divinities operate.

The point here is that since man lives in such a world pervaded by evil spirits, ghosts and their human allies, he is constantly exposed to danger. Since it is the nature of the evil spirits and ghosts to prowl around in search of prey either because they are hungry or in the service of "one's enemies," a person needs to protect himself. No one knows when they will strike; hence he must be ready at all times. Protection can always be found in the form of finger-rings, amulets, wrist bands, and waist bands that have been ritually prepared by "medicine men" or occult specialists. More will be said on this later, but in the meantime it is in order to point out that the Absolute creator of all, including the spiritual and the physical realms, has veto power over his creation. He, however, delegates some power to the spiritual being in charge of each department of his creation; hence he does not always interfere.

Thus, the earth for the typical African is not just a physical reality on which he lives. It is interpenetrated by spiritual forces and, like an onion, has many layers hidden by the outer layer which is open to immediate casual observation. The earth is, therefore, not only mysterious but sacred and impregnated with both good and evil as well as neutral spiritual forces which can be exploited by man.

Man

Man himself is a complex psycho-physical being as mysterious as the earth in which he lives. He is created by God as seen in the myth of creation. As a psyche he is open to God, the divinities, and the spirits as well as the "vital force" on the earth. He is capable of entering into relationship with these entities which may result in good or ill; hence he is very vulnerable to their influences. However, he can manipulate the lower spirits and the neutral force, all of which can harm him if he is careless and does not protect himself against them.

Man has what may be called a tripartite soul consisting of life-force, personality and alter-ego, sometimes called "guardian genius." Others see more than five components of man's soul,[19] but they can be reduced to three to avoid duplication. The "life-force" is given to man by God at conception and it is the part of the soul that animates the physical body. This aspect of the soul can be harmed by metaphysical forces as represented by spirits, divinities and witches. It can also be destroyed by human and natural agents in the form of murder, poison, disease and violence. When any of these entities strikes fatally, the physical body dies.

"Personality-Soul" is the aspect of the soul that does not die. It is prior to the physical body and is created by God. Before coming to birth, each person, in the form of his personality-soul, chooses a destiny which he desires to actualize on earth. This includes the family through whom he will come into the world, the type of job he will do, how long he will live, his status in life and the means through which his demise will be effected. This destiny is then sealed and locked up in the head of the individual, probably in a coded form. Man is responsible to God by means of this aspect of his soul. This soul is also responsible for his character, and it is the part of him that does not perish with the body when the "life-force" is destroyed.

The third aspect of the soul is what we prefer to call the *alter-ego* but which others call "guardian genius."[20] It is, in a sense, a duplication of the "personality-soul" in heaven during the earthly pilgrimage of the individual. Its main duty is to take charge of man's destiny and to ensure that it is actualized. Although the "alter-ego," being purely spiritual, lives in heaven, yet it is immanent on earth to guide the individual. In its immanent form it is hidden in the head of the individual since that is where the individual's destiny is coded. Africans in certain areas of Nigeria, for example, offer sacrifices to their "alter-egos." "A half calabash studded with cowries"[21] may be used to represent the head (as it is done in Yorubaland) or the sacrifice may be made directly to the head (as is done in Edoland).

As already indicated, it is possible for malevolent spirits, witches and wizards, and divinities to make conditions difficult for a person to fulfill his destiny. This is why a man must constantly seek the aid of his "alter-ego," ancestral spirits and divinities to ensure that the unfolding of his chosen destiny is not frustrated by any force. This suggests that a person's destiny is not, strictly speaking, a predestination but rather a blueprint which requires efforts, human and supernatural, to bring it to fruition.

Man's place

At death, (that is the cessation of the "life-force," and hence the physical body) the personality constituent of the soul returns to heaven. This is not always the case as, for example, under certain conditions such as premature death. Should death come before the allotted time, (according to destiny), the personality-soul lingers around as a ghost for some time until the life-span originally given him is completed. Sometimes, the personality-soul of a person who dies before his time in one city may materialize in another distant location where he lives a normal life until his life-span is used up. However, should he be recognized by anyone who knew him prior to his first death, he disappears immediately.

In the case of a person who dies at the right time (which is defined as having been old enough to have children) elaborate funerary rites are performed to ensure his incorporation into the ancestral spirit-world. Soon after his death, the family gathers and invites relatives to arrange for the interment which is the first step in the funeral rites. The corpse is washed, shaved of all hair, the fingernails are clipped and the body is dressed up before being laid in state. In Edoland, for instance, a fowl is killed as a sacrifice. The interment usually takes place within twenty-four hours because of the putrefaction of corpses in the tropical climate. It must be said that this practice of rushed interment is rapidly being discarded because of the introduction of embalming facilities and refrigeration in modern hospitals.

The corpse may be buried within the house, in the courtyard or in a public cemetery; but in modern times the latter is the general rule. At internment various objects are put in the graves: weapons, utensils, food, drink, beads or money. These are meant for the use of the deceased on his journey to the world beyond, and so that he should not appear before ancestors empty-handed.[22]

As a rule, the second phase of the rituals should begin a few days after internment, but because of the expenses involved most people postpone it as long as possible. It must not be too long otherwise the ghost of the deceased, unable to gain admission into the community of the departed members of the family in the absence of a proper funeral ceremony, may haunt the family. This second phase, which may last from seven to forty days, involves several sacrifices, dancing and feasting. At the conclusion of the rites among the Edos of Nigeria, for instance, a special ceremony is held to elevate the spirit of the deceased into the ancestral shrine. This assumes that by virtue of the proper funeral rites the deceased has been incorporated into the community of the departed members of the family. If that is true then it is only logical that this acceptance is re-enacted ritually on earth by symbolically elevating his spirit to the ancestral shrine.

Among the Edos in Nigeria this elevation is carried out in a concrete symbolism. Earlier it was noted that when a person dies the corpse is washed, the hair shaved off and the fingernails clipped. The washing is done with soap and a new sponge. The water used is put in a new clay pot. For the elevation ritual, the fingernails, part of the hair from the head and part of the sponge are moulded with white clay or chalk and kept on the family ancestral shrine. This mode of symbolizing the continuity of the deceased in his relationship with his earthly family is a rich symbolism. It is based on the magical principle which holds that things which have once been in contact with each other continue to interact after the physical contact has been severed. In this case, the presence of the moulded chalk containing the hair, the fingernails and the sponge used to wash the corpse of the deceased constitute the visible embodiment of the presence of the deceased in the midst of his family. Thus death has not dissolved the relationship between the deceased and his family as he can now be invoked at the family shrine.

The ritual cycle of "separation, transition and reincorporation"[23] is completed. The deceased has been ritually separated from the living members of the family through the interment ritual and by means of the proper funerary rites. These rites are believed to help in the process of incorporation into the community of the deceased members who preceded him into the spirit-world. Now, by the elevation or divinification ritual he is reincorporated into the community of the living as an ancestral spirit who, though invisible, is symbolized on the ancestral shrine. In other words, the unbroken communion between the living and deceased members of the family is maintained ritually.

This explains the importance which many Africans place on child-bearing. They believe in an indissoluble relationship between the individual and the members of his family, both dead and living. In fact, scholars euphemistically call the deceased the *living dead* because of the strong belief that even though dead, the unbroken tie with the living remains. Death does not dissolve this union, but if the deceased is not incorporated into the ancestral spirit-community he becomes a ghost. To be a ghost is to be cut off from one's family since a ghost cannot be invoked at the ancestral shrine. As already noted, member-ship in the ancestral community is dependent on character and proper funeral rites. The former is not as important as the latter since everyone thinks that his character is good enough to gain his membership. In any case, the question of character is the sole responsibility of the man during his earthly existence. Proper funeral rites are crucial partly because the individual, at death, does not have any control over it and yet so much depends upon it. For one without children, the thought that no one may care about one's destiny as much as one's children becomes unbearable. Seen from this perspective, it is easy to under-stand why Africans regard childlessness as a tragedy. Only those who are sure that their relatives will care enough to give them appropriate funerary ceremonies can look forward to death with some hope of continuity in the nexus of family solidarity.

PROVISION FOR COPING WITH THE UNCERTAINTIES OF LIFE

A. **Divination**   It is now clear that the typical African sees life as mystery to be lived out on a mysterious earth ruled by spiritual forces of good and evil. There is no event without a spiritual/metaphysical cause; hence man must look beyond physical events to their spiritual etiology. Each man may have a chosen destiny to actualize, but this may be thwarted by malevolent forces which operate either as evil spirits or through witches and sorcerers who are in alliance with them. God may or may not intervene and, in any case, he has made provision by means of which one may deal with life's problems. This is the theodicy of the typical African about evil.

Life, seen against this background, is uncertain; hence man will be wise to avail himself of the divinely ordained provisions for solving the riddles of life and ensuring a measure of certainty. Herein lies the importance of divination in the Traditional Religion complex characteristic of much of Africa. Diviners are people who, by virtue of their extra sensitivity to spiritual reality and years of training, have become "fathers of secrets." They are able to decipher the past, the present and the future – as well as uncover the human and the spiritual causes of events and the possible solution to the problems of life.

With this understanding of the earth and man, it is easy to appreciate the respect people have for diviners and the frequency with which they are consulted. They are consulted about every aspect of life. Parrinder puts it this way:

> If anything is lost, if a barren woman desires children, if there is a mysterious disease, if a man is troubled by strange dreams, and for many other causes, the diviner is sought out and he has recourse to geomancy. The diviner may be called in at all the important crises of life, at birth to discover the appropriate name to give to a child, at the betrothal to find the right husband, at death to find who has caused death. In some places the diviner draws up a horoscope for adolescents, and this is treasured by them the rest of their lives as showing their fate. The horoscope is inscribed on a piece of calabash and any competent diviner should be able to read it. [24]

To the outsider it may seem that divination is nothing but a psychological technique designed to relieve anxiety and give a person confidence to face the vicissitudes of life. There is no doubt that this is one of the functions of divination. But there is so much mystery in life that one must be wary not to reduce every mysterious phenomeon to natural causes. As Parrinder concedes, we cannot rule out the fact that there is undoubtedly some degree of telepathy and extrasensory perception at work at times.[25] Until more knowledge of the divination mystery become available, Parrinder's tentative position appears reasonable. Father Aylward Shorter's investigation led him to a similar conclusion. In his words:

> Some diviners seem to have powers of telepathy because they appear to be able to tell the client facts about himself and the purpose of his visit at the very start of the interview.[26]

Regardless of what scholars may say, for the typical African religionist divination is an important means of unravelling the mystery surrounding the uncertainties of life.

B. **Sacrifices**   Every divination consultation is followed by sacrifices. In fact, since the purpose for consulting a diviner is to obtain a solution to a problem, it is only reasonable to expect that the assumed spiritual nature of problems will necessitate sacrifice as this is the only sure way of communicating with spiritual forces.

Sacrifices form a major part of the religious expression of the typical African traditional religionist. Sacrifices are made to expiate for sins committed, to show gratitude for blessings received, and for permission or license to avail oneself of certain natural facilities like farming and fishing. Other needs may call for sacrifices as well. What we are concerned with here are sacrifices to ward off evil spirits and provide guidance and protection.

Ancestral spirits, as we have already shown, are actively interested in the affairs of their children living on earth; hence they are usually involved in ensuring that their children are protected against evil spirits. Consequently, diviners ask their clients to make sacrifices to their ancestral spirits for protection against fiendish spirits. Divinities are also offered sacrifices for protection. In most cases they are placated by means of sacrifices for the sins committed by the individual as these sins may be presumed to be the cause of his present trouble.

Satan or the Devil is another spiritual being to which sacrifices for protection are often made. Strange as this may be to a Westerner, he has to remember that in the traditional religions found in much of

Africa, the Devil is not the out and out evil being he is depicted in the New Testament. He is more of "a trickster-messenger of the gods, who brings irrationality and confusion into the world."[27] Perhaps, the biblical description of Satan that most nearly corresponds to such traditional African conceptions is that found in the book of Job. There, Satan appears in the assembly of heavenly beings and, in response to God's question, he describes himself as one "who goes to and fro on the earth" or as one who "walks up and down" on the earth. This is why Professor Bolaji Idowu has described Satan as the "Inspector-General" in African traditional religions. Among other things, his function includes the inspection of the appropriateness of any sacrifice made to the divinities.

In addition to this function, Satan can be persuaded to guard one's house from any spiritual invasion. This is why, in most cases, especially among certain ethnic groups, every traditional religionist household has a shrine for Satan at the entrance to the compound or house. There sacrifices are made regularly to Satan to ward off any evil spirit that may attempt to invade the house. In this case, Satan becomes the "bodyguard" of the one who makes regular sacrifice to him.

Malevolent spirits, as we have pointed out, abound and are ready to harm people either out of their own natural inclination or in the service of one's enemies. In order to protect oneself from these, a diviner may prescribe specific types of sacrifices to be made to these spirits. But if they are made in the service of one's enemies it is believed that the sacrifices made to ancestral spirits, divinities and Satan for this purpose ensure that one is protected from attack. In other words, the battle is now shifted from the individual to that between evil spirit and the spiritual forces that are on one's side.

The frequency of such sacrifices is an indication of the seriousness with which people take them as a means of dealing with the mysteries of life. You can hardly walk through any village without seeing, especially at the crossroads as well as at the entrance to the village, signs of fresh sacrifices. In spite of the influence of Christianity and Western sophistication, such sights are not unknown in remote or slum areas of the large cities. As a matter of fact, sophisticated people may offer the same sacrifice in the form of a party known as "sara" which is an Islamized form of sacrifice. The aim is the same, namely, to ward off metaphysical danger. These sacrifices consist of such animal victims as fowls, snails, eggs, and other food items. They are generally inexpensive, however, as the necessity of having repeatedly to offer sacrifices becomes irksome to some. Since no one is certain of when the evil spirits will attack, it is considered wise to comply when a diviner prescribes such a sacrifice for one's protection.

      C. **Protective charms or amulets**   We have already implied that for the typical African the earth is ruled in the main by evil forces who make life unsafe for all, especially the wary. These evil forces work through people who are in alliance with them. Such human agents are usually known as sorcerers and witches. Sorcerers are believed to be more dangerous than witches who operate only at nights. Sorcerers operate both day and night.

      Parrinder has a typical description of what many Africans believe about sorcerers which is quoted in full here:

> The sorcerer deliberately tries to harm his enemies, or those of his clients who have paid him, by evil magical means. He may use suggestive magic only, or true poison. Harmful ingredients may be put in a cooking pot or drinking gourd.... The soul of the enemy may be pinned down with pegs, or a clay image made of his body and thorns stuck in the vital organs. The enemy will then feel pain in those spots and may die....[28]

In a world where this is believed to be a reality, it is easy to understand why life appears unsafe at each moment. If life is unsafe and uncertain because of evil forces and their human allies, are there no good forces and their allies to whom one may go for protection? Traditional religions answer that there are good forces that can be manipulated by their human allies to protect one against the machinations of the evil forces and their mediums.

      The importance of protective charms and amulets for the people of Africa can only be appreciated in the light of their world view as described above. If the world is so unfriendly, then the most reasonable thing to do is to arm oneself against any attack of the nefarious powers. This is why people spend much money acquiring charms which they wear in the form of finger-rings, arm-bands and waist-bands. Some are worn on the wrists and ankles. Besides the ones worn on the body, others are hung on door lintels or buried under the threshold of the entrance to the house to protect against invading spirits. The entrances to villages are also protected by charms hung on the arched entrances or buried beneath the entrances to ensure that any harmful charm brought through or evil spirit that comes through the entrances will be rendered ineffective.

Drivers, fishermen and hunters also commonly wear charms to protect them from curses that may have been placed on their means of livelihood or evil spirits sent after them by their enemies. Parents ensure that their children are well protected from sorcerers and evil spirits by means of the charms they put on them.

In much of Africa this kind of world view is so ingrained in the people that neither intellectual sophistication nor over a century of Christianity has significantly affected traditional practices. It is not uncommon to see highly educated scientists and even many so-called "Christians" protecting themselves through these means, especially in times of crises. It is easy to view it from the outside and say, "It does not make sense; a driver must be stupid to think that a charm hung on the roof of his car will avert an accident." But it does make sense if you recall that for the driver there is no natural event without a spiritual cause. As a matter of fact, for many Africans, there is no such thing as an accident in the real sense of the word. What appears to be an accident is for him, in fact, the result of a spell cast by an evil man or the result of the anger of a divinity whose taboos he has violated. It may even be seen as a just punishment for an evil committed by the driver himself or someone riding with him. Since one cannot be sure of these things, pragmatic wisdom dictates that one should be prepared all the time. This is the reasoning which is characteristic of the African traditional religionist whom we have observed.

In evaluating this aspect of the religious practices of traditional Africans, what Rattray said many years ago (as quoted by Parrinder) is still relevant:

> The labour and infinite pains, the prayers, the spells, the sacrifices, the abnegation, the heart-burning, the disappointments, the hopes that are inseparably bound up in each of these poor fetishes we can only imagine in part, but they should never be quite lost sight of when we are considering such objects, or judging the makers of them. [29]

No one will spend his hard-earned money on something he does not believe has existential implications for his survival in an unfriendly environment. From the viewpoint of the African, anyone who fails to avail himself of protective charms may be likened to an industrial worker who fails to take advantage of the safety precautions provided for his good.

SUMMARY

For the mid-nineteenth century missionary (a great-grandchild of the Enlightenment), from whose world view the dynamic concept of spiritual forces and even God has been eroded, this African world view did not make sense. This lack of empathy for such an African self-understanding was complicated by the missionary's preconceived idea that Africans were so primitive that they did not even have a concept of God. This presupposition made the missionary insensitive to the self-understanding of the African within his world view. Coming from such a quasi-scientific world view the missionary could not perceive spiritual realities in the same way as the Africans he encountered did. His perception of the Africans was that they must be living in a dream world to believe the things they did. Since the concept of God in the African's world view differed significantly from that in the missionary's world view, he was convinced that the African had no concept of God. The missionary was convinced that since the African bowed down to "wood and stones," it was his privilege to introduce the African to the concept of God for the first time. Consequently, the missionary succeeded only in:

> ... preaching to, and in teaching Africans about a strange
> God whom they have somehow come to identify as the
> God of the white man. But what has happened to the
> God... who is the foundation of their traditional belief?[30]

The answer to that question, as Idowu rightly suggests, is that the Church unwittingly left the African converts "with two Gods in their hands and thus made of them peoples of ambivalent spiritual lives."[31] The implications of this will form the basis for the introduction to the next chapter.

Unlike the quasi-scientific world view of the nineteenth century Christian missionary to Africa, the African world view, reflected in the traditional religions of Africa, abounds with notions of spiritual forces.

His entire life is seen in its interaction with these forces at whose mercy he lives his life. Belief in the immanence of God, the creator, is not seen to be incompatible with the notion of God delegating authority to the divinities for the governance of the earth in his thinking. Furthermore, he has provided sources of safety to which man may go for protection against the uncertainties of life. Anyone who fails to avail himself of these helps has himself to blame for any consequences.

The thrust of this chapter has been two-fold. First, it has been contended that there is a world of difference between the quasi-scientific world view of the mid-nineteenth century missionary and that of the African to whom he brought the Gospel. Secondly, it is argued that because of this difference and its effect on perception, the Christian theology formulated in the quasi-scientific world view was bound to be less relevant to the African.

Our analysis of the two different world views reveals certain features which are incompatible. Only a few of these will be mentioned here by way of summary. For instance, while the quasi-scientific world view desacralized the universe, the typical African world view sees the universe as a multi-dimensional entity inhabited by hierarchical cadres of spiritual beings and forces. The earth is seen as an arena where these spiritual beings and forces interact with man for good or ill, depending upon the circumstances. Unlike the quasi-scientific world view and because of its understanding of the universe, the African world view under discussion has no room for accidental deaths and natural illness. It has no natural cause and effect category; every event has metaphysical etiology.

The implications of these differences are many and have tremendous influence on the religious behaviour and practices of scores of Africans. For instance, whereas the quasi-scientific world view makes no provisions for sacrifices, charms and amulets, ancestral-divinity worship, witches and wizards, the world view typically held by African traditionalists makes room for them. The presence of these features in the two world views raises the question of how to formulate Christian theology that is thoroughly Christian and yet takes into account the African self-understanding. The next chapter represents an attempt to answer this question.

4
GUIDELINES FOR A NEW CHRISTIAN THEOLOGICAL APPROACH IN AFRICA

The preceding chapter reveals a world of difference between the quasi-scientific world view of the nineteenth century Westerner and the typical African world view. Our thesis is that given the way context influences one's perception of spiritual reality, such a difference in world view must inevitably affect the resulting theology. In working out the implications of this assumption for the purpose of enunciating guidelines for a new approach to Christian theologizing in Africa, this writer proposes to adapt Segundo's hermeneutical model as a springboard.

In chapter two, we presented the four basic preconditions which, according to Luis Segundo, a hermeneutic circle must take into account. These preconditions, he argues, are imperative if a theologian desires to succeed in enunciating a new way of theologizing that is informed by the appropriate context. The presuppositions underlying Segundo's preconditions may be summarized as follows:

1.   There is a new way of experiencing reality that creates suspicion about the ideological superstructure underlying the current inadequate interpretation of the Scriptures.

2.   Such suspicion, thus aroused, eventually leads to a discovery that the prevailing interpretation fails to take certain vital contextual data into consideration.

3.   The realization of this fact, followed by an act of the will, naturally results in a new hermeneutic that takes the newly unearthed contextual elements seriously.

The question now is to find out if these preconditions for a new hermeneutic are applicable in our situation. Is there any serious observation in the behaviour of the African Christian that suggests a need to re-evaluate the presuppositions of the traditional Christian theological approach? The answer is in the affirmative as reflected in the following observation: *For years many sensitive pastors/theologians in Africa have noticed that in times of existential crisis, the average African Christian reverts to the traditional African religious practices. In some instances, pastors/priests (theologians, if you please) have themselves fallen victim to this almost irresistible reaction to existential confrontation.*

This raises the question as to why these African Christians find it somewhat natural to revert to traditional African religious practices in their attempt to cope with the uncertainties of life as we have described in chapter three.

The mere widespread incidence of this observation arouses suspicion about the adequacy of the ideological superstructure which forms the matrix from which the prevailing Western version of Christian theology was formulated. The suspicion is heightened by the awareness that all theological formulations bear the imprints of the cultural and contextual heritage of the theologians. For this very reason the current theological formulations, having been forged in the North Atlantic context, have not taken cognizance of certain important data, namely, the typical African world view and the resultant traditional religions. This is because, as we have discovered in chapter three, the missionary came to Africa from an intellectual atmosphere that was tainted by the quasi-scientific world view. In that world view only lip-service was paid to traditional Christian perceptions of spiritual reality. This token version of the traditional Christian perceptions, as we have insisted, was, at best, only an afterglow of Christendom that once had vital contact with the spiritual dimension of life. This was vivified by various religious symbols. But by the fourth decade of the nineteenth century such a dynamic orientation to spiritual reality had been radically diluted and replaced with only hollow cliches that lacked the conviction of the former days.

Coming from such a context, and unaware of the presuppositions that shaped his perception of the African self-understanding, the missionary could not be expected to be empathetic in his feeling towards this African world view. Naturally he felt impelled to urge the African to discard his world view. Given the technological superiority of the missionary, many Africans, though only on a superficial level, did what they were told to do. But deep down in the subconscious dimension of their beings, their cultural conditioning remained intact to determine their behaviour in moments of life-problems. From this standpoint it may be said that Christianity was equated, in the minds of these Africans, with Western education and civilization which could be embraced intellectually without existential involvement. In other words, the *Word* did not become *flesh* in the African environment and consequently the Eternal Christ could not be existentially apprehended. In that circumstance, Christianity came to be regarded as a foreign religion that had been transplanted in a foreign soil and did not take root. Consequently, many African Christians perceived the "God" of Christianity as a "stranger-God," the god of the white man, who is unfamiliar with the local spiritual problems. To these Africans, Christianity was of no practical use in times of existential crisis. It seemed much more reasonable to them to revert to traditional practices when faced with serious situations unfamiliar to the God of the white man. Thus, in periods of boundary-situation problems the first reaction of many African Christians is to gravitate towards the traditional religious methods for coping with such crises.

It is this type of reaction, as already indicated, that led Professor Bolaji Idowu to insist that the traditional evangelistic approach in Africa places the African Christian in an ambivalent position. The approach has tended to require the African to pledge a superficial allegiance to the "stranger-God" of the white man who, in his thinking, does not understand his local situation. He accepts this God only intellectually, thus giving the false impression that he thereby denies the God whom he existentially recognizes as the foundation of his traditional religious beliefs and practices. Since old habits die hard, especially in the absence of an existential commitment to a new mode of self-understanding, it is easy to understand why the pull to the old and familiar path triumphs when crises strikes.

There may be a few people, both African and white Christians, who, while conceding that the African world view as presented here might have been true in the nineteenth century, may argue that it is not so today. They may base their argument on the so-called impact of Western civilisation and Christianity. Our answer is that such people are living in *an ivory tower* and out of touch with African ways of thinking and perceiving. It may be good for them to come down to where the action is and mix with the people to learn the truth from them. The experience of a typical African pastor who sits where his parishioners sit during the weekdays is that the world view described here is very much alive today. It determines the very being of the average African no matter what the level of his sophistication may be. It must be conceded that not every African Christian's reaction is determined by this world view. Exceptions certainly exist but they are too few to be of significance or to affect the case made here.

No intention to plead for a revitalization of the world view is intended here. Our aim is, first, to call attention to its existence. Secondly, we want to urge that unless it is recognized and dealt with on the conscious level, the commitment of most African Christians to Christ will continue to remain superficial. For the truth is that this world view is so entrenched in the subconsciousness of even the most sophisticated African scientist that it breaks through every facade of Christianity and Western civilization and comes to the surface in moments of personal crisis. Thirdly, our purpose is to insist that the most honest and reasonable way to handle an existential matter of this nature is not by ignoring or denying it, but by bringing it to the conscious level where it may be shown that Christ is all-sufficient to deal with it decisively. The Apostle Paul's handling of a similar situation in his letters to the Colossians and the Ephesians can be our guide here. More will be said about Paul's example later. In the meantime, our plea is that the theologian should learn from the modern psychiatrist. A psychiatrist does not dismiss his client's anxiety as irrational even when he personally feels it to be so. Instead, he helps the client to unearth the origin of the anxiety by bringing it to the conscious level and then shows him how to cope with it consciously. Regardless of the level of theological understanding of the Christian theologian, if he is to be relevant to a particular people he must first understand their self-understanding.

Our suspicion about the theological presuppositions underlying the formulations of Christian theology in Africa has thus led us to a discovery of the reason behind our observation. Our observation, if you will be recalled, is that in times of existential crisis the average African Christian reverts to the traditional African religious practices. In other words, we have discovered that the Christian theologian in Africa fails to take certain crucial data in his context into account. In consonance with our thesis, this revelation calls for a new hermeneutic that takes cognizance of the elements in the African world view and the resultant religious expressions.

In presenting guidelines for the new hermeneutic, care will be taken to avoid mistakes of the orthodox and liberal theologians which have been so vividly highlighted in David Tracy's analysis which we have already considered. As indicated in chapter two, Tracy attributes the failure of the orthodox theologian to his refusal to recognize that modern man has, indeed, acquired a new mode of self-understanding and approach to reality. The liberal theologian, on the other hand, embraces modern man's claim so uncritically that he feels impelled to reduce the Christian faith to a version which can be communicated within the presuppositional scheme of modern man. The result is that what he does communicate falls short of the Christian faith. This leaves modern man in the lurch, unable to meet his deeper spiritual needs. Pains will be taken to ensure that our guidelines do not lead us to such an error.

In light of the above, it is necessary to reiterate that the guidelines to be suggested are predicated on the assumption that the Christian theologian is one who is convinced that God has acted decisively in Jesus Christ for the total salvation of man everywhere. In addition, the Christian theologian is convinced that man's appropriation of that salvation has validity only as he is existentially committed to the Eternal Christ as manifested in the Jesus of Nazareth. Since every man's perception is influenced by his cultural world view, his apprehension of Christ must inevitably be affected by that world view.

This, perhaps, explains the difference in emphasis in the theologies of various Christian groups through the ages. This historical reality should humble the contemporary theologian. In this regard, the path of wisdom dictates that one listen to Bishop Neil when he declares (the italics are mine):

> The Christian is committed to the view that Jesus Christ is the truth; to the view, that is, that in proportion as Jesus Christ is understood man's understanding of himself and the world in which he lives can be indefinitely extended in the light of the revelation which Jesus gives of God; and that there is no fact or circumstance which intrinsically falls outside that field of explanation. This does not involve the Christian in the claim that other religions bear no relation to the truth at all, *still less in the claim that he himself has apprehended all the truth there is to be found in Christ. But as a believer he does claim to stand in a particular relation to the truth as such and not merely to his own truth.* [1]

In consequence of this stubborn truth there arises a need for the Christian theologian in Africa to pierce beneath the current dogmatic formulation of the Gospel. This exercise will enable him to separate the Eternal Truth from the cultural wrappings in which it had been presented without reference to the African context. What has just been said raises the question of the sources of Christian theology. An examination of Christian theological sources will further explicate the presuppositions of this writer in this enterprise.

The sources of Christian theology may be described in terms of subjective and objective dimensions. Subjectively, the source of Christian theology always remains the Word of God as mediated by the Holy Spirit. Jesus Christ himself underlines this truth in these words: "There is still much that I could say to you, but the burden would be too great for you now. However, When he comes who is the Spirit of Truth, he will guide you into all the truth; for he will not speak on his own authority, but will tell only what he hears; and he will make known to you the things that are coming. He will glorify me, for everything that he makes known to you he will draw from what is mine. All that the Father has is mine and that is why I said, 'Everything that he makes known to you he will draw from what is mine'" (John 16:12–15 NEB). In other words, the theologian must remain tuned into the Holy Spirit, the primary source of theology, as he is faced with any human situation.

The structure of the human mind, we have argued, is such that because man cannot think in the abstract God must mediate himself to man through human beings, material things and situations. This leads us to what we have called here objective sources of theology. Objective sources of theology can be subdivided into primary and secondary segments. The Holy Scriptures, being the inspired book or the primary record of human witness to the divine self-disclosure in history, is the primary objective source for theology. This is what the Church means by declaring that the Bible is the inspired word of God. "For it was not through any human whim that men prophesied of old; men they were, but, impelled by the Holy Spirit, they spoke the words of God" (2 Peter 1:21 NEB). As the inspired words of God, the Bible becomes the 'authentic objective source of the Christian faith. It is, as it were, a divine mirror through which man again and again apprehends God's self-disclosure. This truth is vividly expressed in two stanzas of Mary Ann Lathbury's poem, "Break Thou The Bread of Life." Although this song is essentially intended to point beyond the eucharist to the

Living Christ who gives spiritual nourishment to his followers, yet it points out the place of the Scriptures as a mirror of divine revelation.

> *Break Thou the bread of life,*
> *Dear Lord, to me,*
> *As Thou didst break the loaves*
> *Beside the sea;*
>
> *Beyond the sacred page*
> *I seek Thee, Lord;*
> *My spirit pants for Thee;*
> *O living Word.*
>
> *Oh, send Thy Spirit, Lord,*
> *Now unto me,*
> *That He may touch my eyes*
> *And make me see;*
>
> *Show me the truth concealed*
> *Within Thy Word,*
> *And in Thy Book revealed,*
> *I see Thee, Lord.*

The Holy Bible becomes the primary objective medium by means of which the Living Lord, through the Holy Spirit, continues to disclose God to us. Our theology must, therefore, be authenticated by the Bible.

The secondary objective sources of theology include the Church's dogmatic tradition, human culture and world view, and human historical situations which God uses as occasions for our apprehending his self-disclosure. It must be stressed that these secondary sources must not be over-emphasized at the expense of the subjective and primary objective sources enumerated above. To do this is to miss the whole point. Without the subjective source, namely, the Living Word as mediated by the Holy Spirit, and without the primary objective source – the Bible – as well as the Christian dogmatic tradition, the basis for contextualization is undermined. What is there worth contextualizing if we ignore the primacy of these sources? Any failure to recognize the crucial role of these "givens" in Christian theologizing in Africa will only result in the production of African anthropology rather than African Christian theology.

Having said that, it must be made clear that there is no intention to detract from the importance of contextualization which the guidelines are designed to stress. For as Farley argues, "it goes without saying that theology mirrors its historical situation. This is both inevitable, since historical realities occur in historical contexts and proper, since theology's vocation prompts it to serve its primary community of faith as well as the larger human community."[2] Our thrust has been that while traditional theological formulation bears the stamp fo the historical and cultural self-understanding of its formulators, it has ignored African self-understandings. In other words, Christian theologians in Africa have not come to grips with the hard facts that realities occur in historical context, and that for theology to be authentic and relevant it must be informed by that historical situation.

It has been suggested that the Christian theologian has ignored the African world view for fear that a recognition of it may tend to weaken the faith of the African. An appropriate reply to this type of reasoning is contained in the following statement from the "Study Encounter":

> A strength that is derived from distortion of error, however, is not the strength of Christ, and the time is overdue for a fresh approach to an African heritage that seems to have survived within the Church in Africa despite these attitudes towards it.[3]

With the foregoing background and the consequent challenge to take a fresh look at the African world view in the formulation of doctrinal expressions of the Christian faith, we will now attempt to give a brief analysis of the African world view as presented in chapter three. This exercise will enable us to pinpoint typical elements in the African self-understanding which, in turn, will form the basis for our guidelines. There is no claim that our analysis is not implicit in Christianity itself or other religions for that matter. Our aim is to show that the task of a Christian theologian in analyzing the African context is to unveil an understanding of spiritual realities which, though not emphasized in the Western formulation of Christian theology, is crucial to Africans' existential apprehension of Christ.   These realities are, indeed, present in Christianity but undiscerned by the Western theologian because of the influence of his culture on his perception of spiritual reality. This is what Stephen Neil means when he advises the Western theologian not to despair if his African "partner (in dialogue) sees in him (i.e. Christ) things that I have never apprehended and beholds a Christ in many ways different from the Christ to whom I have given my allegiance."[4] Neil continues to add that "it has been our hope that, when the Hindu and Buddhist turn to Christ, they will convey to us indispensable help in tracing out what Paul so sensibly calls the 'unsearchable riches of Christ' (Ephesians 3:8).[5] What is true of the Hindu or Buddhist converts is equally true of Africans.

TYPICAL ELEMENTS IN AFRICAN
WORLD VIEW AND RELIGION

In addition to the notion of a Creator-God who is transcendent yet immanent in the world, typically the African world-view is characterized by the strong belief that the world is full of divinities, spirits, demons and their human allies in the form of witches and wizards. Thus for the African there is no solid line of demarcation between the sacred and the secular because the spiritual interpenetrates this world. Man is vulnerable and is open to the spiritual forces for ill or good. Consequently, man lives in fear of metaphysical danger and constantly needs the help of spiritual forces for security. This understanding of his world is reflected in numerous practices to ensure a measure of protection from the metaphysical forces that are ranged against him. For him there is no accident; every happening has a metaphysical basis.

This world view also reveals that man can find his real fulfillment only in relation to his human as well as his spiritual communities. This is emphasized in rites of passage which begin with the naming ceremony, followed by puberty rites, marriage, funerary rites and ancestral worship. In each of these rites man is initiated into each stage of life, thus ensuring ritual separation from the previous stage and incorporation into the next stage of life in the bond of a relationship that even death cannot dissolve. This belief in indissoluble relationships is symbolized in ancestral worship. Man is not only related to his human and spirit communities, he is also related to nature. His life is guided by the rhythm and cycles of nature such as the seasons, the phases of the moon and the conjunction of the planets. In fact, as we pointed out earlier, any failure, for instance, to observe the proper rite or procedure in the installation of kings or priests, it is believed, may result in serious repercussions in the processes of nature. These may include drought, outbreak of plague and infertility in women.

The divinities who are regarded as intermediaries between man and God have an important place in the typical African world view. Having been created by God for the purpose of assisting him in the theocratic governance of the world, each of the divinities is believed to have been assigned a specific department of nature over which he had authority, subject only to the veto power of God. When an African worships any of these divinities he thinks he is really worshipping the Creator God through the intermediary. This is why it is argued that underneath the seeming polytheism of traditional African religions lies a monontheistic motif. The Creator God of traditional African religions is the absolute Creator who created both divinities and man. They are all responsible to Him. The conspicuous place given to the divinities in the religious scheme parallels the structuring of the socio-political set up which requires that the king be shrouded in mystery by surrounding him with intermediaries through whom he administers his realm.

Another element in the African world view under discussion that needs emphasis is the role of blood both in terms of its efficacy in effecting reconciliation with spiritual beings and solidarity in the human community. We have already mentioned the importance of blood in our discussion of sacrifice as a means of coping with the uncertainties of life. When an animal is slaughtered as a sacrifice to a divinity or an evil spirit it is done in the belief that the blood of the animal atones for the sin of the worshipper. In human relationships the blood tie is so strong that everybody who can be identified with a particular clan is regarded as a "brother" or a "sister" to other members of the clan and must be treated accordingly. For this reason there is hardly any African ethnic language that distinguishes between the term "brother" and "cousin" as we have in other languages such as English. The only word that refers to blood relationships is "brother" or "sister," as the case may be.

In order to ensure the indissoluble relationship with non-blood relations in African society a blood-oath is taken. To effect this, an incision is made on the bodies of those involved. The resultant drops of blood are exchanged in such a way that a drop of blood from one person enters the body of the other and *vice versa.*Symbolically this means that the people concerned have, thus, become blood relations whose union can never be severed. This also underlines the significance of symbols for the African. In Tilichian language, symbols in the

African world view can be said to "participate in the realities which they symbolize."

This concept of symbol leads us to the fact that the African world view as we understand it, lends itself to the sacramental understanding of the universe. In this everything in the universe is seen as a potential vehicle for divine revelation and mediation. As already indicated, even herbs are said to be capable of being incarnated by spiritual forces for the purpose of revealing their therapeutic potency to the herbalist in the service of mankind. In the same way, the seers, priests and diviners are believed to be able to enter a state of spirit-possession during which they become mediums for divine revelation. Dreams are also interpreted as a divine method of unravelling the mysteries of life to those who are specially tuned into spiritual realities.

There are other elements in the world view and religion that typify much of Africa. Enough has been said, however, to paint a clear picture of the world view that shapes the self-understanding of many Africans. Given a world view in which man understands himself as living in the immediate atmosphere of spiritual forces, many of whom are hostile to his existence, any theology that does not interact with this perception of reality will be irrelevant to those Africans who hold such a world view. Our description of the quasi-scientific world view leads us to the conclusions that it does not lend itself to a sympathetic appreciation of the African world view presented here. Thus, the difference between the self-understanding of the traditional Christian theologian reared in a quasi-scientific culture and that of the African brought up in the cultural conditioning just described is responsible for the latter's ambivalent Christian commitment which invariably waves under existential stress.   The thrust of our discussion has been based on just this point: that because of the orthodox Christian theologian's failure to be informed by the African self-understanding, the average African Christian has remained superficial in his commitment, The superficiality of his faith is betrayed by his reversion to traditional practices in times of existential crisis. In the face of such crises he naturally reverts to traditional religious practices to establish metaphysical security. This being the case, the question arises as to what guidelines may be suggested for ensuring that Christian theological formulations in Africa take cognizance of the African's self-understanding.

Function of the guidelines

However, one more point needs to be clarified before discussing the proposed guidelines; namely, what is the function of the guidelines in the task of Christian theologizing in Africa? This is necessary in order to avoid any misunderstanding. The best way to describe the function of the guidelines is to start by reiterating what has been a consistent emphasis throughout this book. The emphasis has been on the need to distinguish the eternal truths of religion from the accidentals through which those truths are expressed. By accidentals of religion, we mean such things as rituals, temples, sacrifices, liturgies and theological formulations of the experience of the eternal truths. All these accidentals are symbols and models which point beyond themselves to the basic human spiritual needs which cry out for fulfillment.

In other words, both these symbols and the world view which give them form are only vehicles by means of which man strives to concretize his desperate attempts to find solutions to his deeper spiritual problems. Among these deeper spiritual problems are anxiety, sin, estrangement, reconciliation, eternal life, security from demonic forces, spiritual guidance; in a word, salvation understood in a theological context. It is the symbolic nature of the vehicles or accidentals of religion through which these deeper spiritual needs are expressed that justified our earlier use of the term *Messiah* as being the Jewish symbol which points to the availability of God's Saving Presence in Jesus, the Christ. In that case Jesus Christ as the *Messiah* constitutes the embodiment of God's final solution to these basic spiritual problems for whose solution man has yearned through the ages.

Thus, the conviction of the Christian theologian is that this *Saving Presence* of God in Christ is still available to all today. However, the discernment and appropriation of this availability is not necessarily effected through the medium of theology formulated in another culture. This is the case because all perceptions, be they spiritual or otherwise, are culturally influenced. It is in response to this fact that the guidelines are presented as a perspective or framework.

It is our hope that through this framework, the *Saving Presence* of God in the Christ who became *flesh* in a particular historical culture may once again be discerned and appropriated to meet the deeper spiritual needs of man. For the African, the spiritual needs must be defined in terms of his experience and perception through the mesh of his world view and self-understanding. In other words, the features that form the basis of our guidelines are not to be construed as *normative.* They are, therefore, not candidates for belief and Christian commitment. They are presented as a framework within which the discernment of the divine solutions to the basic human spiritual needs may take place against the background of the availability of the divine *Saving Presence* in Christ as presented in the Bible and mediated by the Holy Spirit.

When read against this understanding of religious symbols, the guidelines reveal not merely the universal human spiritual needs for security from demonic forces, reconciliation, deliverance from sin, relief from anxieties, etc., but also those needs which are expressed in African world views. What is crucial, therefore, is not the vehicle through which the African expresses them in the light of his self-understanding. The crucial fact is that the needs are expressed, and hence the Christian theologian is under obligation to show that Christ is able to meet them adequately. Having now clarified their role, we are in a position to offer the following points as possible guidelines for the Christian theologian in Africa who is concerned that the African Christian remains totally committed to Christ through thick and thin.

PROPOSED GUIDELINES

1. A new appreciation of the efficacy of Christ's power over evil spiritual forces

In light of our contention that the African world view is charged with spiritual forces most of whom are inimical to man, the most viable starting point for the Christian theologian in Africa is a recognition of that understanding. This is a very biblical approach in view of the fact that the world view of the first hearers of the Gospel, especially in the Gentile world, was one ridden with fear of evil spirits and demons. Apart from the witness of the four Gospels to this reality, Paul recognized it in his dealings with Gentile Christians, especially in his letters to the Ephesians and Colossians. In his letter to the Ephesians, Paul declares: "Our fight is not against human foes, but against cosmic powers, against the authorities and potentates of this dark world, against the superhuman forces of evil in the heavens." Because to the nature of this struggle, Paul urged the Ephesian Christians to "take up God's armour; then you will be able to stand your ground when things are at their worst, to complete every task and still to stand" (Ephesians 6:12, 13 NEB).

It should be recalled that we have conceded that the Western Christian theologian, speaking from his quasi-scientific world view, could quote this Ephesians passage. Our point is that he could not quote it with the same conviction that led Paul to pen the words to a people engaged in an existential struggle with demonic forces. This he cannot do because his world view does not acknowledge the authenticity of such a self-understanding. As a matter of fact, the Western theologian who quotes this passage with one breath invariably explains it away with another. This he does by saying that such a self-understanding is a relic of ancient superstition which modern man must not countenance. If it is an obsolete superstition unworthy of the attention of modern man, then for the African reared in that world view, the "Christ" of the modern white man must be a stranger to this dimension of existence. Is it any wonder then that in moments of crisis, which he interprets as arising from this dimension of life, the average African Christian does not look to Christ for help?

Let it be re-emphasized that unlike the quasi-scientific world view, the African tenaciously holds that the so-called physical world has spiritual dimensions replete with spirits and demons. These spiritual forces interact with human mediums for the purpose of carrying out their nefarious desires. Consequently, the African lives in fear of those demonic forces and the human allies. In view of this understanding there is a need for the Christian theologian to borrow a leaf from Paul and demonstrate that Christ is not only the all-sufficient saviour from the power of sin but also the all-sufficient conqueror of demons and deliverer from all fears. As Bishop Stephen Neil once succinctly put it:

> Unless the first deliverance from fear has been fully accomplished, unless Jesus has really been enthroned as conqueror of the demons, the believer is still living half in the old naturalistic world in which the spirits have power and the time has not yet come in which his ears will really be opened to hear the teaching concerning sin, righteousness, repentance and forgiveness.[6]

Mere denial or arrogant condemnation of this world view will not be perceived as a valid solution to the problem by the typical African. As far as he is concerned, any authentic Saviour must be capable of destroying the cause of his fears and anxieties. This is why the Saviour to whom he can utterly commit himself must first be the destroyer of evil forces before his saviourhood can be existentially acknowledged. In other words, no religion can be relevant to a people if it neglects any area of their total experience as perceived by them. They will inevitably seek other means to cater for the neglected aspects of their total existence.

2. A new emphasis on the role of the Holy Spirit and the present mediatory efficacy of the Living Christ

If the African finds his fulfillment only in relation to human and spiritual communities, then for him to feel at home in Christianity he must come to a vital appreciation of the role of the Holy Spirit as the unifying force in the Christian community. The solidarity of the Christian community inheres in the power of the Holy Spirit who unites all Christians with God and one another. The Church is the community brought into being by the Holy Spirit by virtue of his indwelling presence in all who are incorporated into Christ. As the one who walks alongside the Christian, the Holy Spirit guides him into all truth, comforts him in times of difficulties, and directs his thoughts as he grapples with the knotty problems of life's decisions.

It is no exaggeration to say that the role of the Holy Spirit has been neglected in Christian theologizing in Africa. This is so partly because the secularized Western theologian is not thoroughly convinced of the reality and hence relevance of the Holy Spirit. He has more faith in psychological guidance than in spiritual guidance for the Christian. The typical African, on the other hand, comes from a world view that lays in store in spiritual guidance which is sought through divination, dreams and sooth-saying. The almost irresistible attraction of the modern pentecostal movement as represented in the Independent Churches in Africa is not unconnected with their emphasis on the place of the Holy Spirit in the life of the Christian. It is not enough to condemn the excesses and the obvious mercenary tendencies of some of these Churches. We must also confess that the failure of the orthodox Christian theologian to put the right emphasis on this verit-able biblical doctrine is responsible for the aberration in its current expression.

The spiritual world is real for the African. He is open to active communion with spiritual forces as he faces the riddles of life. He needs the assurance of solidarity with his human as well as his spiritual communities which, in his traditional world view, are held together by ancestral spirits. In the Christian context, our solidarity with our human and spiritual communities inheres in the Living Christ as mediated by the Holy Spirit. That is to say that Christ, through the Holy Spirit upholds and guides his Church which is his community.

This immediately leads us to the consideration of the present mediatory efficacy of the Risen Christ. Consistent with the implications of his world view that demands that he maintain a vital relationship with the spiritual realm, the African makes regular sacrifices which, we have indicated, are believed ultimately to reach God inasmuch as spirits and divinities are regarded as mediators between man and God.

The orthodox Christian theologian has not taken advantage of this world view to emphasize the eternal and yet contemporaneous efficacy of the priestly role of Christ. For Christ, having once and for all offered himself as the supreme sacrifice for sin, sits in the presence of God, making intercession for us. The tendency of the quasi-scientific world view is to explain away the original theological significance of the sacrificial death of Jesus Christ on the ground that the mention of blood is repugnant to modern man's aesthetic sense.

Sacrifices and mediation may be unimportant to the modern man nurtured in a quasi-scientific atmosphere, but for the African and biblical world views what happened on that Calvary tree has eternal consequences. As the writer of the book of Hebrews expresses it:

> But Jesus lives on for ever, and his work as a priest does not pass on to someone else. And so he is able, now and always, to save those who come to God through him, because he lives for ever to plead with God for them.
> Jesus, then, is the High Priest that meets our needs!... He is not like other high priests; he does not need to offer sacrifices every day, for his own sins first, and then for the sins of the people. He offered one sacrifice, once and for all, when he offered himself (Hebrews 7:24–27 TEV).

The orthodox Christian theologian, no doubt, may read this passage and even preach on it. But its present significance for him has lost the urgency it has for the African who, day by day, struggles with the pressure to offer blood sacrifices. News of ritual killings is not an uncommon occurrence for him. This creates anxiety as he wonders why Christianity as currently formulated does not take into account his self-understanding. How does he reconcile the attitude of the quasi-scientific world view oriented theologian, on the one hand, with the biblical witness to the significance of blood sacrifice and the African world view on the other? From the biblical standpoint, the question of sin is so devastating that God became man in the person of Jesus, the Christ, for the purpose of redeeming man through the shed blood of Jesus Christ.

At the risk of repetition let it be reiterated that the lack of proper emphasis on this aspect of the Christian faith in its current theologizing in Africa, in spite of the obvious clarion call for it, owes its source to the quasi-scientific world view of the Western world. In other words, orthodox Christian theology in its present form, unlike that of medieval Christianity, does not recognize or value the sacrificial and mediatory potency of Christ as being existentially relevant for man today. From all indications these are very relevant for the African as we have pointed out. This again underlines the crucial role of context in one's perception of reality including spiritual reality. The Christian mystic, Bede Griffiths, graphically underscores this in the following statement:

> For centuries now Christianity has developed in a westerly direction, taking on an ever more Western character of thought and expression. If it is ever to penetrate deeply into the East it will have to find a correspondingly eastern form in which the genius of the peoples of the East will be able to find expression. For Christianity will never realize its full stature as a genuine catholicism, that is, as the universal religion of mankind, until it has incorporated into itself all that is valid and true in all the different religions and traditions. [7]

Griffiths' observation has universal relevance and is amply supported by biblical examples which demonstrate that the traditional attributes of God were revealed only as the Israelites confronted the dynamic Yahweh in one human situation after another. That is to say, that God's attributes and what he is to his creatures are open-ended and inexhaustible. It is, therefore, presumptuous for any theologian to hold that his perception of God in a particular context represents an absolute understanding of the living dynamic God, the Creator of the ends of the earth.

Every theologian must make room for a novel perception of God and spiritual reality in a context different from his own. The Christian theologian in Africa must be open to divine self-disclosure within the African context.

3.   A new emphasis on the omnipresence of God and the consequent sacramental nature of the universe

Earlier we implied that the concept of a remote God is an invention of the Westerner who does not understand the extent of the cultural influence on the African expression of his religious beliefs. In that connection we asserted that for the African there is no clear demarcation between the sacred and the secular. He lives in the omnipresence of spiritual realities who, in accordance with his politico-social set up, are *bona fide* vicars of the Creator-God. In that case his worship of them is tantamount to a virtual worship of the Creator-God just as his obeisance to the agents of his earthly king is obeisance to the king himself. That the concept of a remote God is foreign to the African is borne out by his prayers and the meanings of the names he gives to his children. These bear eloquent testimony to his awareness of the omnipresence of God in every aspect of the universe.

In the traditional African world view, whatever a person does or thinks is done in the very presence of God as represented by his spiritual agents. The awareness of this fact, as he perceives it, guides him in his relationship within the society. Consequently, any time he feels that he has violated the norms of the society and the spiritual entities he becomes conscience-stricken. This usually leads to functional and or physical indisposition. He is then seized with an inner urge to confess and make amends. In order to express his inner feelings, he generally consults the oracle by which he is ordered to confess his violations and make sacrifices to atone for the wrongs done or moral norm violated.

Ironically, Christianity has taught the African to regard this traditional awareness of spiritual realities as superstition without emphasizing the omnipresence of the Living God from whom no thoughts and deeds can be hidden. The result is that he now violates moral norms without any compunction because he is not led to believe that God, as presented in Christian theology, is concerned with his "little violations." It is common knowledge that those who desire fidelity in relationships seek traditional religious practices to ensure it rather than depend on the Christian faith to uphold it. This is so because by condemning the traditional awareness of spiritual realities as superstition without the appropriate substitute of the reality of God's omnipresence, the Christian theologian has inadvertently created a spiritual vacuum. The African Christian in this sense is like the man, in the parable of our Lord, from whom an evil spirit was expelled. After wandering for some time the evil spirit returned to find that his place has not been filled. With that knowledge he went to invite "seven other spirits more wicked than itself, and they all come in and settle down; and in the end the man's plight is worse than before" (Luke 11:24–26 NEB).

In order to avoid such a situation, the Christian theologian should take into account this element of the African world which emphasizes the omnipresence of God. In this world view the universe is seen as one huge temple of God which must not be profaned by deeds, words or thoughts since God's eyes are ever open in the persons of his divine agents to what goes on. It is not enough to teach them to turn away from what we like to call "superstitious beliefs." We must analyze what these elements symbolize and guide them to recognize the omnipresence of God and the sacramental nature of the universe to which the world view admirably points. Indeed, this world view reminds us of the truth enshrined in Hebrews 4:13, namely, that "there is nothing that can be hidden from God. Everything in all creation is exposed and lies open before his eyes; and it is to him that we must all give account of ourselves."

CONCLUSION

It is hoped that if these guidelines are taken seriously by theologians in Africa, the African Christian will come to appropriate Christ as the universal Saviour, the "very God of very God" in whom and through whom the whole universe came into being and has meaning. The African will also come to realize that there is no area of human experience that lies outside of the knowledge and power of Christ.

With that understanding the African will have no urge to look elsewhere for security when faced with what he interprets as a metaphysical problem inasmuch as Christ is seen to be all-sufficient for his every need.

Apart from the spiritual benefits that may accrue to the African Christian, the new spiritual discernment from the African contextual perspectives will constitute an African contribution to Christian theology. We have already hinted that Christian theology cannot be universal and full until every cultural group has brought its peculiar perception of spiritual reality to bear on the doctrinal expression of man's apprehension of God through Christ. It is only as the Word becomes flesh in every cultural human situation that the "unsearchable riches of God" in Christ can be approximated, as much as it is humanly possible under the mediation of the Holy Spirit.

The contribution to Christian theology that may emerge from an African awareness of spiritual reality will be very timely for the West. The Western world at the moment is smarting under the pangs of the hollowness and the concomitant anxieties of life which have resulted from widespread secularization. The current renewed emphasis on metaphysics, mysticism, occultism and witchcraft in the West points to a need in man which cries out for recognition. No matter how much or how long man may try to repress his spiritual need by overwhelming it with the glamour of materialism, it will inexorably surge forward for attention. The witness of the biblical as well as the African world view is that life is hollow and incomplete without acknowledgement of its spiritual dimension with all the implications it connotes. It is to make man aware of this that God became man in human history, to show us how to live abundantly and victoriously in a world like this. We ignore it to our hurt and peril.

NOTES

FOREWORD

1. Robert McAfee Brown, "The Rootedness of All Theology," *Christianity in Crisis*, July 18, 1977, pp. 170-174.
2. For a more detailed treatment see Charles R. Kraft, *Christianity in Culture* (Maryknoll, New York: Orbis Books, 1979).
3. See Alan R. Tippett, *Verdict Theology in Missionary Theory* (Pasadena, Calif.: William Carey Library, 1973), pp. 88ff; and *Soloman Islands Christianity* (London: Lutterworth, 1967), pp. 100ff.

CHAPTER 1

1. Ram Desai, quoted on page 124 in *Christianity in Africa as Seen by the Africans*.
2. The consultation was sponsored by the WCC and AACC. Its report was published as item SE/52 in *Study Encounter*, Vol. IX, No. 4, by the World Council of Churches, 1973.
3. Aylward Shorter, *African Christian Theology – Adaption or Incarnation?* (Maryknoll, New York: Orbis Books, 1977).
4. Paul Tillich, *Systematic Theology* (3 vol. in one) (Maryknoll, New York: Harper and Row, 1967), p. 3.
5. Ibid.
6. John Cobb, Jr., *Living Options in Protestant Theology: A Survey of Methods* (Philadelphia: The Westminster Press, 1962), p. 17.
7. Edward Farley, *Ecclesial Man: A Social Phenomenology of Faith and Reality* (Philadelphia: Fortress Press, 1975), p. 3ff.

CHAPTER 2

1. David Tracy, *Blessed Rage for Order: The New Pluralism in Theology* (New York: The Seabury Press, 1975), p. 4f.
2. Ibid., p. 5.
3. Ibid.
4. Ibid.
5. Ibid., p. 23.
6. Ibid., p. 43.
7. Ibid., p. 24.
8. Ibid.
9. Ibid., p. 43.
10. Ibid., p. 44.
11. Ibid., p. 45.
12. Ibid.
13. Ibid., p. 46.
14. Ibid.
15. Ibid., p. 47.
16. Ibid.
17. Ibid., p. 48.
18. Ibid., p. 49.
19. Ibid.
20. Ibid., pp. 51, 52.
21. Ibid., p. 52.
22. Ibid., p. 53.
23. Ibid., p. 35.
24. Ibid., p. 159.
25. Juan Luis Segundo, *Liberation of Theology* (Maryknoll, New York: Orbis Books, 1976), p. 74.
26. W. A. V't. Hoot and H. H. Oldham, *The Church and its Function in Society* (London: George Allen and Unwin, Ltd., 1938), p. 133.
27. Segundo, op. cit., p. 75.
28. Ibid., p. 28.
29. Ibid., p. 8.
30. Ibid.
31. Ibid., p. 7.
32. Ibid., p. 9.
33. Robert McAfee Brown, "The Rootedness of Theology," *Christianity and Crisis,* Vol. 37, No. 12 (July 18, 1977), p. 170.

34. Van Harvey, "What is the Task of Theology?" *Christianity and Crisis,* Vol. 36 (May 24, 1976), p. 119.
35. David Tracy, op. cit., p. 32.

CHAPTER 3

1. Kenneth S. Latourette, *A History of the Expansion of Christianity,* Vol. III, AD 1500-1800 (New York: Harper & Bros., 1943), p. 240.
2. Ibid.
3. Kenneth S. Latourette, *A History of the Expansion of Christianity,* Vol. V, AD 1800-1914 (New York: Harper & Bros., 1943), p. 320.
4. John Miller, *The Disappearances of God* (Cambridge: The Belknap Press of Harvard University, 1963), p. 3.
5. Ibid., p. 6.
6. Osadolor Imasogie, "Langmead Casserley's Understanding of Christian Philosophy as a Basis for Apologetics" (Unpublished Th. D. Thesis, The Southern Baptist Theological Seminary, Louisville, Kentucky, USA, 1972), p. 113.
7. Ibid.
8. Miller, op. cit., p. 6.
9. Carl Becker, *The Heavenly City of the Eighteenth Century Philosophers* (New Haven: Yale University Press, 1932), p. 51.
10. Karl Barth, *Protestant Thought: From Rousseau to Ritschl,* trans. Brian Lozens (New York: Simon and Schuster, 1959), p. 36.
11. Frederick Ferre, *Basic Modern Philosophy of Religion* (New York: Charles Scribner, 1967), p. 159.
12. David Hume, *Dialogues Concerning Natural Religion* (New York: Hafner, 1955), p. 56.
13. Ibid.
14. Becker, op. cit., p. 74.
15. Imasogie, op. cit., p. 130.
16. Imasogie, op. cit., p. 142.
17. E. G. Parrinder, *African Traditional Religion* (London: Sheldon Press, 1976), p. 21.
18. Ibid; p. 119.

19. Olumide Lucas, *The Religion of the Yorubas* (Lagos, Nigeria: CMS Bookshop, 1948), p. 246f.
20. Parrinder, op. cit., p. 136.
21. Lucas, op. cit., p. 249.
22. Parrinder, op. cit., p. 99.
23. Benjamin C. Ray, *African Religions: Symbols, Ritual and Community* (New Jersey: Prentice-Hall, 1976), p. 91.
24. Parrinder, op. cit., p. 120.
25. Ibid; p. 122.
26. Aylward Shorter, *African Culture and Christianity* (Maryknoll, New York: Orbis Books, 1977), p. 136.
27. Ray, op. cit., p. 110.
28. Parrinder, op. cit., p. 117.
29. Ibid; p. 116.
30. Bolaji Idowu, *Biblical Revelation and African Beliefs*, eds. Dickson and Ellingsworth (Maryknoll, New York: Orbis Books, 1969), p. 13.
31. Ibid.

CHAPTER 4

1. Stephen Neil, *Salvation Tomorrow* (London: Lutherworth Press, 1976), p. 34.
2. Edward Farley, "Theological Solipsism and its Therapeutics." (An Unpublished Paper Presented to a Theological Work Group, 1978), p. 13.
3. "The Wholeness of Human Life: Christian Involvement in Mankind's Inner Dialogue with Primal World View" (published in SE/52 *Study Encounter*, Vol. IX, No. 4, 1973, p. 9.
4. Neil, op. cit., p. 37.
5. Ibid; p. 37.
6. Stephen Neil, *Christian Faith and Other Faiths: The Christian Dialogue with Other Religions* (London: Oxford University Press, 1961), p. 148.
7. Bede Griffiths, *The Golden String* (Great Britain: Fontana Books, 1964), p. 174f.

BIBLIOGRAPHY

Barth, Karl. *Protestant Thought: From Rousseau to Ritschl.* Trans. Brian Lozens. (New York; Simeon and Schuster, 1959).

Becker, Carl. *The Heavenly City of the Eighteenth Century Philosophers.* New Haven: Yale University Press, 1952.

Brown, Robert McAfee. "The Rootedness of Theology." In *Christianity and Crisis*, Vol. 37, No. 12 (July 18, 1977).

Cobb, John, Jr. *Living Options in Protestant Theology: A Survey of Methods.* Philadelphia: The Westminster Press, 1962.

Desai, Ram, ed. *Christianity in Africa as Seen by the Africans.* Denver: Alan Swallow, 1962).

Farley, Edward. *Ecclesial Man: A Social Phenomenology of Faith and Reality.* Philadelphia: Fortress Press, 1975.

"Theological Solipsism and its Therapeutics." Unpublished Paper presented to Theological Work Group, 1978.

Ferre, Frederick. *Basic Modern Philosophy of Religion.* New York: Charles Scribner, 1967.

Griffiths, Bede. *The Golden String.* Great Britain: Fontana Books, 1964.

Harvey, Van. "What is the Task of Theology?" In *Christianity and Crisis*, Vol. 36 (May 24, 1976).

Hoot, W. A. V't. and Oldham, H. H. *The Church and its Function in Society.* London: George Allen and Unwin, 1938.

Hume, David. *Dialogues Concerning Natural Religion.* New York: Hafner, 1955.

Idowu, Bolaji. *Biblical Revelation and African Beliefs.* Ed. by Dickson and Ellingsworth. New York: Orbis Books, 1969.

Imasogie, Osadolor. "Langmead Casserley's Understanding of Christian Philosophy as a Basis for Apologetics." Th.D. Dissertation, the Southern Baptist Theological Seminary, Louisville, Kentucky, 1972.

Latourette, Kenneth S. *A History of the Expansion of Christianity*, Vol. III: A.D. 1500-1800 and Vol. V: A. D. 1800-1914. New York: Harper and Bros., 1943.

Lucas, Olumide. *The Religion of the Yorubas*. Lagos: CMS Bookshop, 1948.

Miller, John. *The Disappearances of God*. Cambridge: Belknap Press of Harvard University, 1963.

Neil, Stephen. *Christian Faith and Other Faiths: The Christian Dialogue with other Religions*. London: Oxford University Press, 1961.

Salvation Tomorrow. London: Lutherworth Press, 1976.

Parrinder, E. G. *African Traditional Religion*. London: Sheldon Press, 1976.

Segundo, Juan Luis. *Liberation of Theology*. New York: Orbis Books, 1976.

Shorter, Aylward. *African Culture and Christianity*. New York: Orbis Books, 1977.

Tillich, Paul. *Systematic Theology*. New York: Harper and Row, 1967.

Tracy, David. *Blessed Rage for Order: The New Pluralism in Theology*. New York: The Seabury Press, 1975.

"The Wholeness of Human Life: Christian Involvement in Mankind's Inner Dialogue with Primal World View." SE/52 *Study Encounter*, Vol. IX, No. 4, 1973.